T[...]
OF
SAINT TERESA
OF ÁVILA

THE LIFE
OF
SAINT TERESA
OF ÁVILA

ELIZABETH HAMILTON

Originally published as
The Great Teresa

ANTHONY CLARKE
WHEATHAMPSTEAD, HERTFORDSHIRE

Published by
ANTHONY CLARKE BOOKS, Wheathampstead
Hertfordshire, England, 1982, 1985, *1989*

USA edition: CHRISTIAN CLASSICS, PO Box 30, Westminster,
Maryland, 21157 USA 1985

First published under the title: The Great Teresa
Chatto and Windus Ltd. 1960. Universe Books edition 1963
This edition Anthony Clarke 1982, second impression 1985

© THE DISCALCED CARMELITES OF THE ENGLISH
 REGION OF THE ANGLO-IRISH PROVINCE, THEIR
 REGIONAL SUPERIOR FOR THE TIME BEING AND
 HIS LAWFUL SUCCESSORS

(UK edition) ISBN 0 85650 064 x
(USA edition) ISBN 0 87061 089 9

Printed in Great Britain by
Hartnolls Limited, Bodmin, Cornwall

*La Madre Teresa de Jesús es muy gran mujer
de las tejas abajo y de las tejas arriba muy
mayor*
Mother Teresa of Jesus is a very great
woman as regards the things of this world
and as regards the things of the next greater
still

Words attributed to the Jesuit
Padre Pablo Hernández, a
contemporary of Saint Teresa of Ávila,
Vida de Santa Teresa de Jesús
Francisco de Ribera Capitulo XIII

Por D.O'L.
'hombre de muchas letras'
quien fué la inspiración
de todo este libro

Nada te turbe,
Nada te espante,
Todo se pasa,
Dios no se muda,
La paciencia
Todo lo alcanza;
Quien a Dios tiene
Nada le falta;
Solo Dios basta.

These lines were kept by Saint
Teresa in the breviary she was
using at the time of her death
in 1582.

Be thou by naught perturbed
Of naught afraid
For all things pass
Save God,
Who does not change.
Be patient, and at last
Thou shalt of all
Fulfilment find.
Hold God,
And naught shall fail thee,
For He alone is All.
Translated by Fr. Anselm, O.D.C.

Contents

Acknowledgments

I wish to express my gratitude to Excmo. y Rvdmo. Señor Don Santos Moro Briz, Bishop of Ávila; also to the many Discalced Carmelites who did so much to help me during my travels in Spain—especially R. P. Eulogio de San Juan de la Cruz, Prior of La Santa, Ávila; the Prioress and nuns of the convent of the Incarnation, Ávila; R. P. Román de la Inmaculada of Salamanca; R. P. Pedro de la Inmaculada of Valladolid and R. Fr. Luis de San José of Burgos. I am also greatly indebted to Señor Don Antonio Villacieros Benito, Director General de Relaciones Culturales in Madrid; Mr. Arthur Montague of the British Council in Madrid; Profesor Alfonso Gamír y Sandoval of Granada University; Profesor Emilio Orozco Díaz of Granada University; M. Patricia Dwyer, Colegio de la B. V. María, Madrid; Señores de Bardaji of Arenas de San Pedro; Señores de Svarbi of Madrid and Ávila, and Señor Don Rafael de los Ríos y Gómez de la Granja formerly of Ávila.

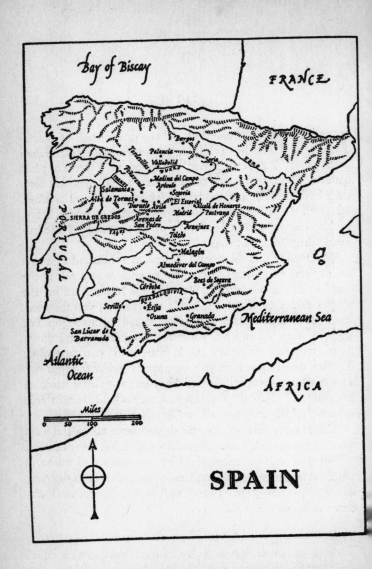

Bay of Biscay

FRANCE

Burgos

Palencia
Valladolid
Tordillas
DUERO
Soria

Peñaranda
Medina del Campo
Arévalo
Salamanca
Segovia
Alba de Tormes
Duruelo
Ávila
El Escorial
Alcalá de Henares
Madrid
Pastrana

PORTUGAL
SIERRA DE GREDOS
Arenas de
San Pedro
Aranjuez

TAGUS
Toledo

Malagón

Almodóvar del Campo

Córdoba
Beas de Segura

GUADALQUIVIR

Sevilla
Écija
Granada

Osuna

Mediterranean Sea

San Lúcar de
Barrameda

Atlantic
Ocean

AFRICA

Miles
0   50 100   200

SPAIN

I

Ávila

I CAME to Ávila in the dusk. There was a smell of wood-smoke, and the echo of children's voices from under an arched gateway. A shepherd passed, wrapped in a brown plaid blanket. Then, two black oxen pulling a high wooden cart; their bells tinkled, and the heavy wheels jolted and creaked. Snow on the ground made luminous patches of white. It lay, too, against the curve of the walls where they bulged into immense drum-shaped towers.

You lived within these walls, Teresa, as a child and a girl. At twenty-one you went out of them to enclose yourself in the convent of the Incarnation. You left the Incarnation for the stricter enclosure of Saint Joseph's, the convent you founded. Your life seemed to have ended. Yet, it had hardly begun. For thirteen years, on and off, you were travelling up and down Spain, under scorching sun and in bitter cold. You were often ill, often tired; sometimes you were lonely. Some thought you a saint. Others were scandalized: they said you were mad, an impostor, a gad-about. You saw visions, yet held them of little account, asking only to walk in Christ's way of humility.

Within forty years of your death you were canonized with your countrymen Ignatius, the soldier and Isidro, lover of oxen.

Teresa in heaven, enlightened by the unclouded vision of God, help me here in Ávila, and on my journeys through Spain, to see you as you were on earth, that seeing the woman I may come to know the saint.

*   *   *

There was snow. Yet in the brilliance of the morning light I saw that the winter was past. The buds bursting on the poplars

13

made a haze of gold that seemed to enclose each tree, like a
nimbus round a saint. There were the storks, too. They soared
on silk-white wings above the city's towers, and sat up awk-
wardly in nests of sticks piled high on the belfry of Santa Ana.
This convent looks like a fortress, with its tiny barred windows
set in enormous walls. Teresa used to visit it, to see her friend,
María Vela, who was a nun there. In it, too, when Teresa was
sixteen, the boy who was to become Philip II of Spain watched
the clothing of three of his mother's ladies-in-waiting and was
himself, to mark the end of babyhood, ceremoniously attired
in breeches.

From Santa Ana I followed a twisting, quiet street. A donkey
laden with little fat milk-churns in baskets was going along it
unattended, stopping of its own accord from door to door.
There was another behind it straddled with sacks full of loaves.

I came, presently, to the Plaza de Santa Teresa flanked to the
east by the ancient Romanesque church of San Pedro, built of
stone the colour of a dried apricot, with beside it two acacia
trees taller than itself. In front of this church there are little
heraldic lions carved in granite, looking like cubs that had been
turned to stone in the middle of their play. In the centre of the
plaza, near a statue of Teresa wearing the habit of a Carmelite,
men in black corduroy with lean sun-grooved faces, that might
have been cut out of wood, were talking to a priest who wore
his cloak flung round him like a Roman toga. Beyond them,
dwarfing all else, and caught in the full light of the sun, were
the walls, as golden-pale as a sheaf of barley.

I had come to Ávila at the time of year in which Teresa was
born. March 28th, 1515, is the date recorded by Don Alonso
Sánchez de Cepeda in a book in which he used to put down the
birthdays of his children. It is mentioned, too, in the *Processes*
for her canonization, where she is described as a native of
Ávila, of well-born parents. The Duke of Navas is quoted as
saying that her lineage was more ancient than his own.

Her parents' home was in the Plazuela de Santo Domingo,

now the Plaza de la Santa, on the site of the seventeenth-
century Discalced Carmelite monastery which has Teresa's
coat of arms carved upon it. I tried to imagine what this house
must have been like, re-creating it in my mind from the *palacios*
or mansions of the nobility that I saw in so many of the streets.
The Cepeda home may not have been as imposing as some of
these, but it cannot have differed greatly, for the town houses
of the well-born were built to a pattern. Immense solid walls,
bearing upon them the family escutcheon, fling their black,
clear-cut shadows on to cobbled streets or squares planted with
little twisted elms. Windows, some surmounted by a classical
pediment, are small and barred. A wooden nail-studded door,
with a smaller door cut into it, opens under an archway into
a *patio* with, perhaps, a colonnade and a fountain and a mass of
flowering shrubs. Inside, a stone staircase sweeps up into darkness. Spacious rooms open one into another. Ceilings are
carved and painted in the Moorish style. The Cepeda mansion,
like many others, was near to one of the city gates. There is a
saying in Ávila: '*Una puerta, un palacio*', for a palace was, first
and foremost, a stronghold charged in time of war with the
city's defence. When Teresa was writing the *Way of Perfection*,
the palaces of Ávila provided her with an illustration of what a
contemplative convent should be; a fortress manned with a
chosen company of the King's soldiers.

The history of Ávila is one of siege and fighting. *Ávila de los
Caballeros*, they call it. Ávila of the Knights. Its men were
renowned for their courage. The Duke of Alba, commanding
the armies of Philip II in the Netherlands, granted leave to his
troops from Ávila in recognition of their bravery. From early
times it was the privilege of the soldiers of this city to carry their
flag in the forefront of battle. Here, again, Teresa's imagery
comes to mind: 'Let the contemplative consider what he is
doing, for if he lets the standard fall the battle will be lost.' Nor
were the women less fearless than the men. Teresa must have
been familiar with the story of Ximén Blázquez who, in the

absence of the men, led wives and daughters, disguised with
beards and masculine garments, in a triumphant onslaught
against the Moors. Moreover the pride of this people equalled
their courage. When the Emperor Charles V visited Ávila in
1534, he was required to bare his head and, having kissed the
cross, swear to respect the liberties of the citizens.

The whole of Teresa's life was a period of war and unrest.
Spanish troops were fighting in France, Italy and the Netherlands. In 1520 Luther burnt Pope Leo X's bull *Exsurge* in the
presence of the students of Wittenburg. Life was held cheap
whether by Philip, Catherine de Medici or Elizabeth of England
who decorated the façade of her palace with the heads of her
enemies. Hardly twenty years before Teresa's birth, Christopher Columbus had offered Ferdinand and Isabella dominion
over the recently discovered America. The shadow of war fell
on the New World, too. Five of Teresa's brothers took part
at the battle of Iñaquito in 1546. Eleven years later, one of them,
her beloved Rodrigo, was killed in an engagement against the
Araucanians in Chile. With such a background and with a
military tradition on both sides of her family, it is not surprising
that again and again she urges her nuns to acquit themselves
like good and faithful soldiers: that, thinking, too, not only
of the city's climate but of its Spartan courage, she speaks of
herself as inured to the rigours of Castile.

Even the cathedral at Ávila is a fortress, its apse forming a
curve in the city walls that rise so naturally out of the rock on
which they are built that it is hard to tell where rock ends and
walls begin. It is austere, yet luxuriant in the grandeur of its
gilding and marbles, its stained glass and carving. Indeed, no
building better reflects the spirit of Castile—the spirit, too, of
Don Alonso de Cepeda, a man stern in self-discipline who yet
took pleasure in his crimson and violet doublets and his shirts
embroidered with gold. I remember the cathedral on the vigil
of Easter: the Paschal candle moving up the aisle, its flame
flickering in the vaulted darkness; the great doors creaking in

sudden gusts of wind; the dank cold rising from the flagstones.
In Teresa's day the congregation used to bring with them a little
metal ball, called a *bolilla*, filled with hot water. She sent one
from Toledo as a present for her brother Pedro, when he
returned from America. 'He is in church so much,' she writes,
'that his hands must get cold.'

*   *   *

In the charters of Alfonso XI mention was made of a certain
Vasco Vázquez de Cepeda as having helped the King in the war
over Gibraltar. This Vasco settled later at Tordesillas, near
Valladolid, where he built a house close to the church and left
instructions that he should be buried on the gospel side of the
altar. One day, when happening to pass through Tordesillas, I
tried unsuccessfully to find his tomb. I saw instead some beautiful Moorish cloisters, and at the foot of the town the Duero's
tawny flood. I also saw a young owl with ruffled feathers
perched, in broad daylight, on the steps of a church, blinking
its eyes.

There were three branches of the Cepeda family, descended
from Vasco Vázquez. One lived at Tordesillas, another at
Segovia, a third at Toledo.

Teresa's father belonged to the Toledo branch, many of
whom were merchants of distinction. The family moved,
however, to Ávila where at nineteen Don Alonso married
Doña Catalina del Peso by whom he had two, if not three,
children. After her death he married Doña Beatriz Dávila y
Ahumada, Teresa's mother. Doña Beatriz was fourteen at the
time of her wedding, her husband fifteen years older.

Don Alonso was a man of courage, integrity and strict
truthfulness. It was said of him that he was never known to
speak ill of anyone. For me, he lives not only from the picture
Teresa has left of him, but also because I see in him the qualities
that were in my own father. He was proud yet gentle, kind to
his servants, compassionate towards all in distress. Unlike many

of his contemporaries, who had captive Moors in their household, Don Alonso could not bring himself to own a slave. Once, when for a while he was looking after a slave-girl belonging to his brother, he treated her like one of his children: the thought of her not being free caused him deep distress.

He was a great reader. His library included Boethius' *De Consolatione Philosophiae*, Cicero's *De Officiis*; the *Proverbs* of Seneca, the works of Vergil; a *Life of Christ in Pictures*, by Juan de Padilla; a *Treatise on the Mass*, by Diego de Guzmán; the *Great Conquests beyond the Sea* which was then particularly popular, as well as contemporary poetry.

Doña Beatriz was also a reader, but she liked the romantic tales of chivalry, then in vogue, about heroes and fabulous monsters, knights and their ladies—such books as the *Amadís de Gaula* which shocked the moralists, but had delighted the young Ignatius of Loyola. She let her children read these, too, to keep them from worse things. In Teresa's case the reading of romances became an obsession. She read day and night, was never happy unless there was a new one. All this, as far as possible, was without Don Alonso's knowledge, for he disapproved strongly.

It was not that Doña Beatriz was frivolous. Quite the contrary. Teresa says that, though her mother was extremely beautiful, she took no account of this; that, when she died at the age of thirty-three, she dressed like a woman already advanced in years. Moreover, she was pious and careful to bring up her children to be the same—encouraging them in prayer and in devotion to certain of the saints. She was a person who had suffered greatly. Her childhood had been darkened by the deaths of her father and her brothers, while in her married life she was constantly ill. Her reading was an escape. She read, Teresa says, to forget her great trials. She has come down to us, through her daughter's writings, as tranquil and highly intelligent, yet a phantom creature, removed from the world of her husband and children.

Behind the Carmelite monastery at Ávila there is a little garden where, they tell you, Teresa, when she was a small child, used to play with her brother Rodrigo, who was four years older than herself. They were fond, too, of reading a book called the *Flos Sanctorum*: a collection of lives of the saints published in Spanish at the beginning of the century. There are two copies in the Carmelite convent at Valladolid, written in stiff Gothic lettering and illustrated with wood-cuts showing the bloody deaths of martyrs—many of them women—at the hands of fierce, turbanned Moors. Sometimes the devil is there in the form of a horrible negro, just as Teresa saw him years afterwards in the convent of the Incarnation. It is easy to imagine the impression made on a child by such pictures; the more so as she was hearing, all round her, talk of wars fought in the name of religion, and Spaniards being killed by Moors, Lutherans and American Indians.

The idea came to her that she, too, would like to be a martyr. Not, she emphasizes, from any conscious love of God, but because here was a quick way of attaining to the joys which, she was told, were stored up in heaven. Eternity had taken hold of the children's minds: the thought of pain and glory that would last for ever. They used to talk of this and chant the words: '*Para siempre, siempre, siempre!*' For ever, for ever, for ever!

Determined, then, to be martyrs they resolved to beg their bread to the land of the Moors. Leaving the city by the gateway in front of their home they dropped down from the walls to the south-west, then crossed the five-arched Roman bridge over the Adaja's stony course. Ahead was a fierce countryside, strewn with granite boulders—the haunt of brigands, witches and warlocks. They were following the Salamanca road. Yet, to the children Salamanca meant nothing. Their hearts were set on the *tierra de Moros*, a distant land not marked on any map but real because it lived by the fire of their imagination—where, dying for Christ, they would win eternal bliss. However, they had gone only a short way when they were met by one of their uncles on horseback—the episode is depicted on a window in the Carmelite church—who, without further delay, took them back to their mother. Doña Beatriz, distraught with terror, already imagined them at the bottom of a well. She reproached Rodrigo as being the elder. '*La niña* made me do it,' he retorted indignantly.

Years later at the giving of evidence for Teresa's canonization some witnesses made much of this episode, as though the five-year-old child was already a saint. Yet, if they seem to have exaggerated the importance of what one may be inclined to dismiss as no more than a childish escapade comparable in another age with playing at pirates or Red Indians, these seventeenth-century admirers of Teresa realized that already the pattern of her life was set, her goal determined. In the child we see the woman who, once she has conceived an idea, cannot rest until she has put it into practice, whom eternity alone can satisfy.

Unable to attain martyrdom, the children played at being hermits. They used to build themselves houses in the garden. But they were baulked in this, too, for the stones they piled up fell down again. Sometimes, if she was with girls, Teresa pretended to build a convent or to be a nun. There were moments when she thought she might like to be a nun. But it seemed dull as compared with going to the land of the Moors.

*   *   *

Teresa was thirteen when her mother died. She says she was twelve or a little less. But she had no head for dates: she did not think them important.

'When I began to realize what I had lost,' she writes in the *Life*, 'I went in my distress to an image of the Virgin, and with many tears besought her to be a mother to me.' The gentle, beautiful Doña Beatriz had been an ethereal creature: an invalid withdrawn into a world of the imagination fostered by her romantic reading. Teresa loved her; but it was, I suspect, with that instinctive, dutiful and partly idealistic love which a child can feel for a parent, rather than that more deep and rare oneness of spirit which was always there uniting herself and her father, however much this might seem to have been disturbed by some passing circumstance. For Teresa the death of Doña Beatriz was the final withdrawing of her mother. But the distance was there already, and could only have increased with the years.

'When I began to realize . . .' The realization came to her gradually—the strange chillness of life, day by day, without a mother. Instead, María, her stepsister, had assumed authority unsurely and therefore, one may guess, a little aggressively. There was the bleakness, too, of a home deprived of its mistress. Teresa was slow to comprehend. Then the full impact came upon her, suddenly—a loneliness she had not known before. And, with that instinct that was hers all her life to better a situation rather than lament it, she betook herself to the hermitage of San Segundo on the outskirts of the city and in contemplation of an ancient statue of Christ's mother, which is now in Ávila cathedral, she was comforted.

*   *   *

I stood one evening in the dim light of the cathedral looking at this statue of la Virgen de la Caridad. In the glimmer of the tapers the dark eyes stared down at me. The smile was stiff, like the smile of a doll. The white brocade dress stood out like a bell. I thought of Teresa, the child, weeping for her mother. Then I went out along a street that twists past the shop where they sell *las yemas de Santa Teresa*—cakes that are like a bun with a whole egg in the centre—and, from there, under the arch of the Puerta del Alcázar into the *plaza*. Even before I arrived I could hear the roar of voices, for it was the hour of the *paseo*. There was a swarm of people. Those who were not walking up and down sat at tables outside Pepillo's restaurant, sipping their sherry or *cerveza* or coffee or just talking. Black-coated waiters summoned by a clapping of hands (this was how the Moors used to attract the attention of their servants) moved among them, balancing trays. I took my place at a table with my friends; the grave yet humorous Virgilio and Pilar his plump, good-looking wife. Pilar was fanning herself with a graceful turn of the wrist: she had the serene expression of a woman to whom life is deeply satisfying. But it was the young girls who held my attention: the two daughters of Virgilio and Pilar, and others besides. They were handsome rather than pretty. All of them had ear-rings and their hair was neat and smooth. They wore lipstick, but with discretion, and a touch of powder. As they moved, their bright, crisp dresses made patterns like petals thrown upon the air. They went in groups, three or four together, arms linked, chattering, laughing, whispering. There was about them that touch of sophistication that means childhood is left behind but not far behind. It was something in the swing of a skirt, the turn of a head. While still in their cradle they had basked in the admiration of a strict but adoring father. Now, they had begun to bask in the admiring glances of dark-eyed, golden-skinned young men. The girls and the young men were mostly apart, keeping to their own groups. Sometimes the groups mingled. When this was so, it meant, as a rule, that they were related. My Spanish friends and acquaintances had, I discovered, numerous relatives. Indeed, I had the impression in Ávila that everyone to whom I was introduced was cousin to everyone else.

Again I thought of Teresa. She was fourteen, or perhaps fifteen, now; grown-up for her age; with dark, sparkling eyes under arched brows. Years later, when evidence was being given for her canonization, an old nun in the Incarnation remembered her as a girl wearing an orange skirt trimmed with black velvet galloons. She took trouble with her dark, wavy hair, and small pretty hands. She used perfumes galore—anything, in fact, that was likely to enhance her charms. In a letter

written to her brother Lorenzo, in 1562, when she was forty-
seven, she recalls this period: 'I kiss my brother's hands a
thousand times for what he sends me. If the medallion had
come in the days when I wore gold ornaments, I would have
coveted it dreadfully, for it is extremely pretty.'

She spent much time in the company of cousins who were,
she says, almost exactly her own age or a little older. It used to
be thought that these were the children of her uncle, Don
Francisco de Cepeda, who had a house adjoining his brother's.
It has been shown, however, in a recent study of Saint Teresa,
that Don Francisco's children were too young to answer to
Teresa's description; the cousins[1] to whom she refers must have
been the three sons and daughter of Doña Elvira de Cepeda,
Don Alonso's wealthy sister whose name is coupled with his
own in documents of the day and who was the widow of
Hernando de Mejía, a prominent citizen of Ávila. The sombre
Cepeda mansion in the Plazuela de Santo Domingo, made yet
more sombre by a mother's death, had begun to echo with
laughter and gaiety. Don Alonso, it is true, felt some misgivings.
He did not wholly approve of the upbringing of his sister's
children, who were more given to worldly pleasures than his
own. Even so, he could not shut the door on them. Teresa, on
the other hand, was delighted with the cousins, and they with
her. She listened enthralled to the tales of their escapades and
flirtations and amused them in turn with her witty conversation
and her sharp repartee. It was the fashion for conversation
among the 'young set' to be smart—a little daring. Gallants
boasted of their conquests, girls of their admirers, love letters
and assignations.

She had reached the age when restraint becomes irksome,
when she felt it a right to choose friends of her own. She chose,
in particular, a relative older and more sophisticated than
herself. It may have been Inés de Mejía, Doña Elvira's daughter.
But this is no more than guesswork. We know, only, that it was

[1]See Appendix, p. 182.

someone whom Doña Beatriz had tried, without success, to keep from the house, fearing the effect of this relative's frivolous conversation upon the young Teresa. After his wife's death Don Alonso had tried too, but with no better result—there were too many reasons for her coming. María, also, joined in. But her scoldings only drove her stepsister the more into the company of the friend of her choosing. It was one of those intense, emotional friendships that young girls are prone to. Teresa was always in the company of her friend, gossiping, listening to gossip, being initiated into pastimes she had not known before—into a world that had little in common with that of the Don Alonso's household.

A friendship of this kind is absorbing but not exclusive. It is fed upon an exchange of confidences, especially a recounting of love affairs. Teresa had fallen in love and, in her friend, had a confidante more worldly wise than herself. She does not say in so many words that she fell in love. But that alone makes sense of the accusation she brings against herself of having exposed her father and brothers to danger. An indiscreet word or act, however innocent, on the part of a girl or her admirer was enough to cast a slur on her honour. In such a case a male relative would feel bound to take up the gauntlet, with the result that it was a common thing for blood to be shed in defence of a girl's good name. In the choosing of a friend opposition had only goaded Teresa on. In her first experience of love it was the same. She let discretion go to the winds, deceived her father, connived with the servants. She had become, in her own eyes, one of the heroines of the romantic novels to whom, in the field of love, all is fair and opposition only an incentive to daring. Who was it, we may ask, that Teresa loved? Again, as when trying to identify the older relative, we are in the dark. There is, however, a tradition that there was one cousin whom, alone out of her numerous relatives, she resolutely refused to see in later life. Was this the young *hidalgo* whom she had loved as a girl?

In some autobiographies the backward look is remote, analytical; the writer views his past with detachment, as though it were not his own. Teresa does not write in this way. The account she gives of her adolescence is charged with emotion. Words rush out pell-mell. From time to time, too, the sequence of thought is broken to make some judgment across the distance of the years. She blames herself bitterly for having deceived her father, for having allowed the servants to encourage her in wrong-doing, for her vanities and frivolities. She says that from her friend she learnt all manner of evil— that parents should see to it that children at an impressionable age keep virtuous company. Then she says it was not her friend who is to blame, but herself—her own evil nature. There are hints and ambiguities. She wrote the *Life* at the order of her confessor. A constraint was put upon her. She was forbidden, she says in the preface, to write in detail of what she calls her wickedness. Left to herself she would have shouted the truth from the housetops. The truth, she used to say, never hurt anyone.

Teresa's self-reproach is excessive. It runs like a motif through the *Life*. 'If I had not been so wicked,' are the opening words. She contrasts her wickedness with the goodness of her parents and brothers, her impiety with the piety of the nuns in the Incarnation. She is a worm, a worthless creature, deserving to be in hell with the devils. This is something that goes beyond the humility of the saints, the realization of their unworthiness in the face of their Creator. Teresa, the saint, had this humility —but there is much, besides, which is part of Teresa the girl and the woman and is independent of her sanctity. Her self-reproach must be seen against the background of her country, her times and her upbringing.

It can be explained to some extent, I believe, as a camouflage, assumed as unconsciously as the tiger's stripes or the dried-wood markings on the plumage of an owl. To use self-depreciatory language was the surest defence against carping clerics—

especially the Inquisitors, who were always waiting to swoop on anyone guilty of what they were pleased to regard as a lack of humility, particularly a woman who, in any case, was by divine dispensation (so they thought) a witless and unstable creature. To be a woman at all in sixteenth-century Spain was, as Teresa puts it, to feel your wings droop. The attitude of the day is illustrated by the statement of Padre Jerónimo Gracián, her friend and Superior, that a manuscript she wrote on the *Song of Songs* was burnt at the order of her confessor merely because he thought it 'a dangerous innovation' that a woman should presume to touch on such a subject. It is a significant fact that in the innumerable private letters written by Teresa to her friends there is little trace of this self-deprecation.

'If you look at Castile, you will understand our saint.' The speaker was a Carmelite father I met in the train between Madrid and Ávila. The skin was drawn tight across his forehead and cheek-bones, as though he had lived exposed always to scorching sun or shrivelling wind. From her earliest years Teresa had looked from the walls of Ávila on to a landscape of savage boulders and treeless plain reaching away to where the mountains stood, sharp as a flint-edge, upon the skyline. The winter was bitter, the summer heat without mercy. The light was hard, shadows black and clear-cut. There were no half-tones, no softness. It was the landscape that helped to mould a people to whom life presented itself in extremes. *Todo o nada*. All or Nothing. Heat or cold. Light or darkness. Truth or falsehood. God or the devil.

The truths of the Catholic Church are unchanging, but the emphasis can vary from country to country, age to age. The Spaniard broods on the more sombre truths of the faith; sin and the fruits of sin, death and the judgment. In the dark churches of Spain scourged and bleeding Christs, Nazarenes in purple robes and bowed beneath the weight of the cross, brass-crowned Virgins with tears upon their cheeks, bear witness to God's love, but still more to man's sinfulness. Sin and penance are in the foreground. Any Catholic church, whatever the country, has, I suppose, its pious women who, if not engaged in good works, may be seen sitting there at any hour of the day, like birds who have found themselves a comfortable roosting-place. In Spain women of this kind—they are called *beatas* and many of them wear a simplified religious habit— have a peculiarly tense, purposeful look and live lives much given to penance. I remember in Córdoba a lady who on a blazing July day apologized to me for wearing a black woollen dress. Later she told me that she did this as a penance in fulfil- ment of a vow she had taken.

If this is so now, it was more so in Teresa's day. As if to compensate for the indifferent and often evil lives led by both laity and religious, there were excesses in matters of penance and mortification. Teresa's health did not allow her to resort to the extremes indulged in by many of her contemporaries, nor in the convents she founded did she encourage her nuns to do so. She said repeatedly that obedience to God was better than penance. Nevertheless, she was Spanish enough to be impressed by the austerities practised by her friend Peter of Alcántara. She was impressed, too (but also amused), by the *beatas* of Villanueva de la Jara, eccentric ladies, worn to skin and bone, who recited Divine Office out of discarded breviaries no two of which were alike. Another person whom she admired— though less on account of her penitential life than because such a life had not made her vainglorious—was Doña Catalina de Cardona, for a time governess to Philip's son, Don Carlos, a lady of ducal family who among her many eccentricities signed her letters *La Pecadora*, lived in a cave, fed on roots and leaves and wore, over a hairshirt, a garment which made her look like a man. She was moreover visited by the devil in the form of a mastiff.

The circumstance, too, of Teresa's childhood conditioned her to a sense of guilt. Her father, whom she loved and admired, was rigidly truthful. Her mother, whom she also loved, deceived her father, reading behind his back the forbidden tales of chivalry and encouraging her children to do the same. Teresa speaks of her mother's small fault: *aquella pequeña falta*. But the mention of it shows how large it loomed in her memory. To us Doña Beatriz's subterfuge seems a trivial one, but to a child deception between parents is not trivial. 'Don't tell your father' or 'Don't tell your mother' are among the most disturbing words a child can hear. Besides, Teresa instinctively sympathized with her mother; it was from her she had inherited her imagination, also her sociability. Don Alonso was by nature something of a recluse; Doña Beatriz had become one only through force of circumstance. Because Teresa was in sympathy, she sensed her mother's guilt and, as a child does, took it unconsciously upon herself. As she grew older she shared more deeply in this guilt, becoming an even greater reader of romances than her mother.

Her sense of guilt, exaggerated by the conflicts of adolescence, followed her into later life. It shows itself in a diffidence that at first sight seems surprising in one who is otherwise courageous and enterprising. 'I am always timorous when I have to make a decision about anything—I immediately think I am going to do everything wrong,' she writes from the Incarnation when she is Prioress in 1573. Often when she has achieved something in the face of difficulty and opposition, she suffers a reaction, begins to question the wisdom of what she has done. This happened after the founding of Saint Joseph's and again at Medina del Campo. This weakness in Teresa is a very human one. It is a reminder, too, that those whom the Church has raised to her altars as great servants of God, heroic in courage and singleness of heart, are yet persons like ourselves. The saints will not please the cold perfectionist nor the stoic. They are not supermen, flawless, nor beings changed once and for all by a lightning conversion. Saint Paul's conversion appears to have been a lightning one, if any was. Yet in the years that followed he was buffeted by an angel of Satan, nor is there any reason to suppose that he ceased to be buffeted to the end.

A person suffering from a sense of guilt can be cured, or at least made better, through treatment from a psychologist; or through a change from unfavourable environment to favourable. In either case the part played by encouragement is all-important. Teresa, though in her spiritual and active life she had much to discourage her, found encouragement, too. When all were against her, thinking her a mad woman and deluded by the devil, Peter of Alcántara encouraged her. Possibly that strange character, as remote from our understanding as one of the desert hermits and the last person one would expect to take up a woman's cause, was himself encouraged by the young Teresa who, so she tells us, took an interest in his affairs. She was encouraged, too, by the Dominican, Vicente Barrón, Don Alonso's confessor and afterwards her own, who, when she had given up prayer, saved her from the slough of false humility, making her understand, what she was later to pass on to others, that to pray is always good, nor is any soul, however evil, excluded from the love of God.

Teresa's self-depreciation, her preoccupation with her own worthlessness, had its roots in natural causes, but it was redeemed through her sanctity. As self was forgotten and God became all, her sense of guilt was swallowed up in something greater than itself: humility. This virtue on which she dwells continually in her writings is not self-abasement, a feeling of inferiority, diffidence or timidity, but an acceptance of things as they are. Humility, she says in the *Way of Perfection*, is nothing else than truth. And again in the *Interior Castle*: 'To be humble is to walk in truth.' The soul that is humble knows that it exists only because the hand of God holds it in being minute by minute; that without God all that the world can offer is of no more worth than 'a few twigs of withered rosemary': *unos palillos de romero seco*. Yet this is not a cause for gloom—no one disliked gloom more than Teresa. ('May God defend me,' she says, 'from gloomy saints.') 'What we must do,' she writes to her brother Lorenzo in 1576, 'is to flee from all to the All'; *lo mejor debe ser huir de todo por el Todo*. It is the teaching of her contemporary Saint John of the Cross. Only by emptying itself of all can the soul attain the All that is God, in whom all that has been relinquished is found anew;

> *Quien a Dios tiene*
> *Nada le falta;*
> *Solo Dios basta.*

* * *

At Ávila within a few minutes of the Plaza de Santa Teresa there is the garden of San Roque. Children play there under the fir trees calling to each other in excited nasal voices, and betrothed couples sitting side by side on the stone benches stare demurely in front of them. Below is the plain and on the far horizon mountains that in early May are still sheeted with snow. By moonlight the plain becomes a sea of opal and the mountains immense black islands—the Lofoten islands as I saw them once in the dawn making a wall across the sea. It is a view with which Teresa was familiar from childhood. She looked out at it, too, later in her life when she went to live at Saint Joseph's, the first convent of her Reform, which stands on high ground to the north of the garden and in her times was not as now shut in by buildings and high walls.

Below the garden to the east a road drops down to where the royal monastery of Santo Tomás stands like an outpost on the very fringe of the city—indeed, one is scarcely any longer aware of the city. In summer a hot wind blows in from the plain bringing with it grains of tawny dust and a desert smell of herbs and parched earth. In the courtyard in front of the monastery swallows twitter and sheep nibble the scant grass. The simple approach gives no idea of the splendour within; the elegant cloisters, and the church in which the altar is supported by an almost horizontal arch raised so high above the ground that the Mass becomes a drama enacted on a stage swung between earth and heaven. In the Capillo del Santísimo Cristo—where there is an immense crucifix not strikingly realistic as are many in Spain, but of tremendous power and serenity—a tablet on the wall records that here on the feast of the Assumption in the year 1562 Teresa saw the Virgin and Saint Joseph in a vision of such dazzling brightness that by comparison all things on earth were as a smudge of soot. She came many times to this church, for she held the Dominican friars in high esteem—among them, Padre Vicente Barrón, 'a Consultor of the Inquisition and a very learned man'; Padre Domingo Báñez to whom she turned for advice in matters both spiritual and material and Padre Pedro Ibáñez, professor of theology, at whose order she wrote the first draft of the *Life*.

Coming back once from Santo Tomás in the golden evening light, I followed the tinkling of ox-bells into a narrow, lion-coloured street that ended in the tiny Plazuela de Vacas, where there is an ancient, battered hermitage and a drinking trough with a few pillars, one of them carved with the Moorish acorn design. Oxen stood there with great slobbering mouths and black angular bodies that looked like wooden boxes covered with hide. A yellow dog ran among them, inconsequently.

Continuing from here through a maze of streets with half-doors like cottages in Ireland, I came upon a building huddled under the walls of the city, as if it had been left to doze undisturbed through the centuries. Two stone pillars supported a shabby whitewashed porch with above it barred windows that seemed to blink at me from under the golden-red of a tiled roof crowned with a belfry. Above the belfry a sky weirdly streaked with lilac, turquoise and jade was crowded with the black, scything wings of swifts dipping and swerving and filling the evening with shrill, bewildering cries. It was the convent of Our Lady of Grace, where Teresa was sent as a pupil in the spring of 1531.

Teresa says that she was her father's favourite: *la más querida de mi padre*. He loved her so much that he found it hard to see any fault in her. Even so, he was not blind. He decided, however, to bide his time. The opportunity came when his daughter, María, married Martín de Guzmán and went to live at Castellanos de la Cañada, about forty miles from Ávila. Now that there was neither a mother nor an elder sister at home, it would have been considered unfitting for a girl of almost sixteen to continue living in her father's house.

The convent of Our Lady of Grace goes back to the year 1507, when a certain Doña Mencía López, widow of a silversmith in Ávila, decided, along with her daughter and two friends, to live the life of a religious in her own home near the church of Santo Tomás. The following year, the Bishop gave her a hermitage dedicated to the saints Justo and Pastor, close to some houses that had belonged to the Moors. Doña Mencía bought these, which were later altered to become the present building. To supplement the community's meagre income, girls from well-born families in Ávila were taken as pupils. They slept, under the supervision of a nun, in a dormitory lit by a lantern, and had lessons in the great thick-walled room with a brick floor and two small windows that is now the sacristy.

For the first week Teresa was unhappy. She was restless, and made more so by the fact that her friends outside tried to unsettle her by sending messages. Besides this, her Castilian pride was hurt—her honour, the thought of which used to be a torment to her. She felt that people were talking about her, were aware why she was there. Then she settled down, even to the extent of admitting that she was happier than she had been in her father's house. For four years she had been without a mother. To a large extent she had gone her own way, made her own friends, but it had brought upon her the disapproval of her father and scoldings from María. As a result, she had been in a conflict. In the convent, where there was no question of continuing her former friendships, she soon ceased to want what she could not have. Instead of disapproval, she found herself made much of by the nuns; for wherever she was, God, she says, gave her the grace to please people. She liked listening to the conversation of Doña María de Briceño, the nun in charge of the dormitory—a woman of intelligence who had been inspired to take the habit after reading the words 'Many are called but few are chosen'. She used to watch the nuns at their prayers, and was impressed if she saw one of them weeping. Mistaking emotion for religion, she imagined this to be a sign of virtue and felt guilty because she could read the whole of the Passion without shedding a tear. Perhaps it was at the convent of Our Lady of Grace that she picked up the habit of weeping all too easily. In many of the crises of her life, she could do nothing, she says, but weep.

After eighteen months in this hothouse atmosphere she fell ill and returned to her father's home. She was again in a conflict, for her future was facing her. Was it to be the cloister or marriage? Neither pleased her. Teresa was attracted by romantic love as presented in the tales of fiction. Given a different background, different influences, she might well, with her charm, intelligence and sympathy, have made not only an important but also a happy marriage. As it was, romantic love seemed well enough, but she saw marriage only in terms of Doña Beatriz. She had watched her gifted and beautiful mother withdrawing more and more into a world of make-believe from a life that was not so much unhappy as drab. She had seen her die worn out with child-bearing, the cares of a family and prolonged illness. Teresa confessed that she feared marriage. For the explanation there is no need to look further than Doña Beatriz.

If she feared marriage, she was repelled by the religious life. It is true that the atmosphere of Our Lady of Grace had worked on her emotions. She had even thought of becoming a nun, then thrust the idea from her. The piety she saw round her

seemed excessive. Like the girl in a song of her own century.
She did not want to be a nun:

¡No quiero ser monja, no!

Teresa went to Castellanos de la Cañada to convalesce from
her illness at the home of her stepsister. On the way she broke
her journey at Hortigosa to visit her uncle Don Pedro de
Cepeda, the widowed brother of Don Alonso. I made a detour
there one day when returning from Alba de Tormes to Ávila.
The road was rough and desolate, the plain tawny as a desert or
golden-brown with stubble. On the edge of each village
we came to there was a threshing-floor where the harvested
grain stood in great yellow piles. Sleek black oxen were treading out the corn, and chaff flung from the winnowing-fan fell
in a shower of gold. I remembered that Teresa, in a letter to
Padre Gracián, describes how one day on her travels, when she
was resting by a heap of grain, a salamander from out of the
corn ran up her arm between the tunic and the flesh. Her
brother Lorenzo snatched hold of the creature and flung it from
him, but it caught Antonio Ruiz, who was one of the party, in
the mouth.

Hortigosa is in a valley, in a fold of the *sierra*. On one side
there is sloping ground planted with black holm-oaks, and
below, on the far side, a stream bordered with willows and
poplars. You could scarcely call it a village—a mere handful of
tumbledown hovels on either side of a track so rough that it
was painful to walk on. There was a church with a cock-eyed
belfry crowned by a stork's nest. An old countryman touched
my arm with a hand that was like a bird's claw. '*La Santa
habitaba allí,*' he said. '*La Santa,*' he repeated proudly, and
the faded eyes glowed. He was pointing to the only building
of consequence; a fine stone house, standing apart.

Teresa used to read to her uncle out of his dry theological
books. They were not at all to her taste, but to please him she

put a good face on it. As she read, and still more as she listened
to the conversation of this stern *caballero* who was to end his
days as an Hieronymite friar, she felt again the awareness of
eternity that she had experienced as a small child; the realization, too, dear to the Spanish heart, that the world is vanity
and soon to pass; that all, except God, is nothing. She thought
again of becoming a nun. But the idea was still repellent. And
yet she knew that something was drawing her.

The conflict lasted for three months, during which she
suffered from fainting fits and attacks of fever. Towards the
end of this period she began to read the letters of Saint Jerome
which had been recently translated into Spanish. The fierce
austerity of the writing came to her like a challenge: '*Dime,
caballero delicado, ¿qué haces en casa de tu padre?*' The blood of the
caballeros was in her veins. What indeed was she doing in the
house of her father?

She made her decision and, in making it, did violence to
herself. The arguments she used had their roots, she says, not in
love, but in fear and expediency. To be a nun, she told herself,
was the safer course. The life of the cloister would be purgatory, but purgatory could be endured if at the end there was
heaven—heaven immediately. She was still the child ready to be
martyred by the Moors if martyrdom would win celestial
joys more quickly.

Don Alonso had been troubled by his daughter's flippant
ways. He was more troubled now. She was his darling, his joy
and comfort. He could not consent to lose her; he would listen
neither to her nor those who pleaded on her behalf. The most
he would say was that after his death she might do as she wished
—but not now.

Her mind was made up, to all intents and purposes her honour
pledged. There could be no going back. And yet she knew that
if she waited she might weaken. So, determined that she would
get her way if not by one means then by another, she stole out
of her father's house in the chill November dawn of All Souls

Day 1536 and in the company of a younger brother, Antonio,
made her way on foot to the Carmelite convent of the Incarnation half a mile to the north beyond the city walls. So great
was her distress that it was as if the agony of death could not be
greater. Her bones seemed to be wrenched asunder. Nor
could she feel any love of God to console her for the loss of
kinsfolk and father.

2

The convent of the Incarnation

I LIKED to stand on the ramparts of Ávila in the shimmering August midday, when there was no sound but the cicadas' sleepy chorus. Beyond pantile roofs and olives and pale parched earth I saw the convent of the Incarnation standing there, brown as cinnamon, with its belfry and great buttresses, and garden walls that sweep back like the wings of a bird.

Heat of this intensity has the power to annul time. The past becomes present and the present past. I had felt this in Jerusalem and Jericho, and asked myself if this is why philosophies and religions so often have their origins in the east. And now it was the same in Ávila. Without any effort of will or imagination I was back in Teresa's century. Or was it that she had come forward into mine?

A sandy road dropped down past cottages with vines growing against them and gardens bright with carnations. Old women making lace sat in the doorways. They used to smile and call out greetings in cracked voices. Then there was a little humped bridge over a stony watercourse with, to the right, a patch of walled-in ground where a horse was tethered. At this point along the road there was always a smell of straw and farm animals. Presently, the convent was facing me, partly hidden by elm trees with thickened, dust-coated leaves. Boulders jutted out of the ground. I liked to sit for a while on one of these and look back at the city walls following the ups and downs of the hills; at this distance the turrets were like castles on a chessboard.

A door opened into what seemed to me like a stable yard. There was an acacia tree in it, and hollyhocks and a few hens scrabbling in the dust. From here I went into the convent porch. Porch, at least, is the word by which the Spanish *zaguán* is usually translated into English. In fact, it is an outer hall, like the *vestibulum* of a Roman house. When Teresa founded the convents of the Reform, it was usual for the Blessed Sacrament to be reserved in this porch until a chapel was ready.

The floor was cobbled, the walls whitewashed and set into one of them was a plain wooden cross painted a faded mulberry-red. A bell and a tangle of ropes hung from the dark, beamed roof. Facing me as I came in was the ancient door, studded with nails, through which Teresa had entered that November morning, and, on a line with this, the 'turn'—a revolving wooden contraption built into the wall, by which letters and other objects can be passed into the convent without the nun on the further side being visible. There used to be a continual coming and going at the 'turn' of the Incarnation: people bringing notes or gifts or asking for prayers, or visitors wanting to see the chapel or relics.

*   *   *

I heard lowered voices, the clinking of keys and the scraping of bolts. The door swung open. Presently, I heard it close behind me.

Four nuns were standing so as to form a square. They wore brown habits made of a thick, rough material. Black veils hid their faces. I noticed their bare feet in the hempen sandals.[1] They gathered round me, greeting me in Spanish and asking questions. Then they lifted their veils. One of them was laughing. I heard a voice speaking to me in English. It came from a nun I had not noticed before. She wore the white veil of a novice, but her round pink face was not young. Later I learnt that she was over sixty years of age, formerly a *marquesa*, a widow and the mother of ten children. Behind the nuns I was conscious of white walls and on one of them a charcoal drawing

[1]See Appendix, p. 182.

of Christ at the Pillar. There were many dark, ancient paintings, some of them in gilt frames. One was the picture of the Samaritan woman at the well, and under it the words *Domine, da mihi aquam*, which Teresa had brought to the convent from her father's home.

The Incarnation is shabby, but it has an air of grandeur. Not the grandeur of such a convent as Las Huelgas, the burial place of kings outside Burgos, but grandeur nevertheless. Or perhaps it is not so much grandeur as elegance, space and light. It is true that some of the rooms are small and have low ceilings, and that there are dark passages and staircases. Yet I am left with a prevailing impression of light. I remember the golden sunlight streaming through the cloister's brown-shuttered windows, then breaking on the white walls and the red-tiled floor. There are two spacious cloisters, an upper and a lower; two white-walled choirs rich in paintings, baroque gilding and statues of saints and Virgins dressed in brocades or embroidered velvet and crowned with spiked glittering haloes.

Everywhere there are reminders of Teresa. This, I was told, was her chair. This, the crucifix she brought with her from Toledo. Here she saw the angel that transfixed her heart with a shaft of gold. Here Peter of Alcántara appeared to her after his death. At the foot of the stairs, legend tells, the Christ child spoke to her. At the top, Christ bearing his cross told her not to be wearied; he, too, had been weary. Again, a legend? In a life filled with visions and ecstasies, in which one mystical experience follows close upon another, where is one to draw the thin line that separates objective truth from allegory, allegory from fantasy? There are those who say that the cupboard in the cell that was hers during the years that she was Prioress gives out a delicate fragrance. I smelt nothing, unless it was the dry scent of old wood. Am I, then, to conclude that others are deluded? What of the witnesses who one after another in the *Processes* for her canonization gave evidence of the fragrance given forth from her body after death? There is, too, an accumulation of similar evidence, some of it doubtful, some difficult to dismiss as untrustworthy, in the lives of numerous saints. Teresa herself, writing of the strange Catalina de Cardona (not a saint), whom I have mentioned earlier, says that the nuns in the Toledo convent, one and all, remarked on the fragrance that clung to her habit and girdle. There was the case, too, of the Archbishop of Valencia, Saint Thomas of Villanove, who died in 1555. When his tomb was disturbed twenty-three years later, during alterations to the church, the whole building, it is said, was filled with a beautiful perfume.

The Incarnation owes its origin to a certain Doña Elvira González who, in the latter years of the fifteenth century, decided, along with other pious women, to live the religious life under the protection of la Virgen del Carmen. A picture in the Incarnation, going back to its early days, shows this Virgin with her white cloak spread about her sons and daughters of the Carmelite Order. Later a convent was built, where the first Mass was said on April 4th, 1515, the day on which Teresa was baptized, in Ávila, in the great dark parish church of San Juan.

The present building, which is believed to have been converted from a farm, has the character of a nobleman's country home. It stood close to what had formerly been a synagogue. In Teresa's day the valley round the Incarnation was said to echo with the lamentation of Jews driven out of Ávila the previous century.

Originally there were to have been not more than fourteen nuns, but the number increased rapidly. Seculars, too, found their way in, on one pretext or another. When Teresa was asked to come back as Prioress she insisted that these should be removed. As to the nuns who were in the convent when she herself entered it is true that she speaks of their piety. Yet remarks she lets fall are more revealing than she meant them to be. She says that, despite her many faults, she was not guilty of talking through crevices or over walls at night. Let parents be warned, she reiterates. Better that girls marry far below their station (a fate terrible in her day) than to be in convents where, thinking to escape the world, they find themselves in ten worlds at once, in which youth, sensuality and the devil conspire to lead them into evil. At home evil ways are found out. In a convent they remain long concealed, while meantime the corruption spreads. Girls in this unhappy plight are, Teresa says, to be pitied; they have nowhere to turn, no means to escape. Often they do only what they see others do round them.

There were nuns who lived useful and holy lives. But there were also innumerable women who from the spiritual standpoint ought not to have been in a convent at all. They were there because there was not anywhere else for them to go. Some had been left widows. Many had been put there by their parents. Fathers of good birth had not necessarily the money to provide their daughters with an adequate dowry. Anyway, there was a shortage of men in consequence of the wars and the attractions of the New World. There were girls, too, who had been unfortunate in a love affair or whose reputation had been tarnished. For the latter a convent was an honourable place of refuge; as the Mayor of Zalamea remarked, the Lord was not over-fastidious as to his brides. Even the hierarchy were concerned at the superfluity of religious, which partly explains the difficulty Teresa experienced in obtaining licences to found the convents of the Reform.

The life that was led in a fashionable convent such as the Incarnation was not a strict one. The nuns were allowed to stay away on visits, sometimes for a considerable stretch of time—this, in fact, was encouraged, as it cut down the expenses of the community. Teresa, because she was intelligent and had a pleasing personality, was much in demand among her friends and relatives; witnesses in the *Processes* for her canonization repeatedly give evidence of her gracious manner and her gaiety: *suavidad y alegría*. At one time, she writes, she was hardly ever in the convent. This is borne out by her biographers, Ribera

and Yepes, who both say that before the founding of Saint
Joseph's she spent over three years at the home of her friend
Doña Guiomar de Ulloa, a rich widow whose mansion in
Ávila is still standing.

The religious habit was worn, but it was usual to crimp the
coif into fetching shapes and to wear brooches and bracelets,
necklaces and rings. Hence the macabre reminder from a
contemporary moralist that the cloister is a tomb and 'jewels
ill-becoming to a corpse'. Moreover, the prestige of a nun
depended less on her piety than her dowry. Those who brought
little were relegated to sleep in a dormitory. Teresa, on the other
hand, who was well provided for by Don Alonso, had a pleasant
cell and off it a kitchen and a guest room. After her father's
death she was able to have her younger sister, Juana, to live
with her at the convent until the latter married. She also had an
oratory which she decorated as she pleased with pictures and
statues. It was customary for a nun, if she could pay the expenses, to celebrate in her oratory the feast of her favourite
saint—a practice that Teresa admits having observed with
'more vanity than spirituality'. The celebration often took the
form of a musical party, to which friends were invited.

There was, too, an interminable coming and going of visitors
in the *locutorio*, or parlour. Relations and townspeople came,
bringing their visitors with them. Young gallants, fascinated
by the unattainable, stared longingly through the grille. One
made such a nuisance of himself that Teresa, then Prioress, said
she would get the King to cut his head off. Perfumed notes,
verses, gifts of candied fruits, sweet potatoes and other delicacies
from the New World were slipped through the bars. Conversation ranged over such topics as the campaigns in Flanders and
elsewhere, the Lutherans, literature, music and even Platonic
love. The *locutorio* was, in fact, a salon, where elegant ways of
speech were cultivated.

The spiritual life was at a low ebb. Such vitality as it had
tended to show itself in hysterical devotions, bouts of exag-

gerated penance and false mysticism. There were innumerable false mystics, some of them nuns without a vocation or *beatas*. A few were conscious frauds, others the victims of hysteria. Magdalena de la Cruz, the Poor Clare from Córdoba, after deluding the Inquisitor, Alonso Manrique, as well as the Empress Isabella, at whose request she had made the christening robe for the child that was to be Philip II, admitted to being an impostor and to having entered into a pact with the devil. There was also the *beata* of Piedrahita, who boasted that she lived always in the company of the Virgin whom she used to wave into a room before presuming to enter herself. As intelligent a man as the mystical writer, Luis de Granada, was taken in by a woman purporting to have revelations. At Ávila John of the Cross was called in to exorcize a nun at the convent of Our Lady of Grace who claimed to give divinely inspired interpretations of the Scriptures. He was also consulted by Teresa in the year 1573 over the crazed Isabel de San Jerónimo whom he diagnosed as suffering from melancholia—a complaint that appears to have been as common as 'nerves' are today. Better, Teresa writes, to found no convents than to have them filled with melancholic nuns. She attributes the 'interior trials' of her cousin María Bautista to an 'over-active imagination' (brought on by melancholia), and in the *Interior Castle* gives warnings against so-called mystical phenomena which take the form of constrictions in the chest, violent sobbing 'like the sobbing of children', blood gushing from the nose and other such 'disconcerting symptoms'.

The shallow, unsatisfying life lived in many of the convents was not one of luxury. If the nuns' thoughts turned too readily to the dainties given them through the grille, it was because often they had not enough to eat. When Father Juan Bautista Rubeo, the General of the Carmelite Order, visited the Incarnation in 1567, he forbade any more novices to be received for fear they might die of hunger. At that time there were a hundred and eighty nuns, but their dowries were inadequate for the upkeep of the large house and grounds. Walls were crumbling, snow and rain leaked through the chapel roof. It was a sordid poverty, fostering discontent and joylessness.

Yet whatever faults there may have been in the Incarnation, it is there, I believe, more than anywhere else, that the spirit of Teresa has lived on. She founded the other convents, stayed in them and went away again. In the case of Saint Joseph's, she was there for about four and a half years. But she lived for twenty-seven years in the Incarnation, and that does not include the three when she was Prioress. In it she suffered, struggled, faced and resolved her conflicts, set herself at last upon the way on which she was to change from an emotional unstable girl into a mature woman and a saint.

I felt at home in the Incarnation. If I found myself in Ávila today and followed the sandy road past the cottages and, over the humped bridge—if I clanged the bell in the cobbled porch, it would be the same; of this I am certain. I was welcome whether I exchanged no more than a greeting at the 'turn' with a being known to me only as a voice; whether I talked through the grille of the *locutorio* to nuns who looked like the Carmelites in Poulenc's opera; or whether the great wooden door swung open to admit me into the white-walled enclosure.

The chapel at the Incarnation, enlarged since Teresa's time to include the cell that was hers those twenty-seven years, is an imposing building with a high-domed roof, ornate gilding, marble pilasters, and, on the floor, the words: *La tierra que pisas es santa*. The ground on which you stand is holy. Yet, I was less moved by this than by the knowledge that the chalice which John of the Cross held in his hands is used to this day in the Mass.

What moved me perhaps most was the upstairs room, scarcely changed since Teresa's day, which was her cell when she came back as Prioress in 1572 with orders from her Superiors to reform the convent. She had come back reluctantly to 'this Babylon', as she calls it, 'this hurly-burly' (*esta baraúnda*) where she had herself lived a life by no means reformed; knowing, too, that among the nuns there were many who were her contemporaries. When the moment came for the Provincial to bring her into the chapel, her supporters began to sing the *Te Deum*. There were others, however, who tried to bar the entrance, shouting in indignation and claiming their canonical right to choose their own Superior. The uproar could be heard from the walls of the city. She was too intelligent not to know that a high-handed manner would achieve nothing nor was it in keeping with her nature. The next morning, when the community assembled in the chapter room, they found her sitting at the feet of a statue of la Virgen de la Caridad. 'I have come,' she said, 'only to serve'. She had as chaplain the thirty-year-old John of the Cross. '*Un padre que es santo,*' were the words with which she introduced him. A year later, an ecclesiastic who made a visitation declared that the atmosphere in this crowded convent was as peaceful as at Alba de Tormes, where there were only a dozen nuns.

It would be wrong, however, to think of Teresa's problems at this time as being only on the spiritual level. Not least among them was how to feed the community. In a letter to a friend, Señor Maldonado Bocalán, she expresses her regrets that, because she had not his address, she could not ask him to send some fowls he had offered: 'So great are the needs of this house and of the sick nuns that they were wanted very badly.' In another letter she asks her sister Juana for turkeys.

I remember Teresa's cell in the half-light of a summer evening. Two twisting pillars, belonging to a small altar set up in the saint's honour, gleamed like golden sugarsticks. On a line with these was the cupboard that I mentioned earlier. At right angles to this a deep-ledged window, about a foot and a half above the ground, looked on to a cloister with, on the far side, brown-shuttered windows through which I could see tiled roofs and tree-tops silvered by the wind. Sheep were bleating and there was the smell of hay.

Nada te turbe,
Nada te espante,
Todo se pasa,
Dios no se muda.
La paciencia
Todo lo alcanza . . .

The words echoed through my mind as though carried upon the soughing of the wind.

*　　*　　*

Nada te turbe. The woman who wrote the lines I have quoted had travelled a long way from the young girl who exchanged her father's home for the convent of the Incarnation. The young Teresa was at the mercy of her emotions. The religious life, she says, was a delight to her. Even to sweep a floor gave her joy. Yet she was often in tears. She was weeping, she explains, for her sins but she gave others the impression that she was discontented. Moreover, a rebuke caused her the greatest distress, especially if she thought it unjust. She could not bear, either, to appear ridiculous. She wanted to be thought well of in everything. When she had to intone an antiphon in choir, she did this badly, partly because she had not practised as she should, but more because, having no musical gifts, she dreaded to make a fool of herself. When she ceased to worry she did better.

She says, too, that she wanted to acquire patience—though she must have had more than she imagined, to bear as she did with an old nun who was suffering from a particularly repellent complaint. The desire was good, but its expression theatrical. She prayed that she herself might be afflicted with the nun's illness, if in this way she should attain her end quickly. From that time she suffered increasingly, from headaches, fever and the mysterious sixteenth-century complaint described, vaguely, as 'heart trouble': *mal de corazón*. Indeed, all who knew her were alarmed, specially Don Alonso. Pious biographers like to see

Teresa's illness as sent by God in answer to her prayer. If the illness of the nun and her own are to be related, the most I would concede is that Teresa's preoccupation with the illness, along with the false assumption that suffering is necessarily conducive to patience, disposed her, in that highly-strung phase of her life, to fall ill more easily: in short, that God allowed natural causes to take their course.

Teresa's illness reminds me of Natasha's, after she ended her engagement with Prince Andrei. The doctors, Tolstoy says, while busy labelling and treating each symptom, were baffled because the source of the illness was in a sphere beyond their reach or comprehension. Even today, the relation between mind and body is only beginning to be understood. It is impossible, then, across the distance of four hundred years, to assess with any degree of certainty the nature of Teresa's illness, particularly as it has come down to us, not in the detached record of a medical casebook, but in the colourful and sometimes macabre account given by herself and her biographer, Ribera. The symptoms suggest hysteria, but they are said to be equally those of malarial fever, which was rampant in the Spain of her day. Whatever name be attached to the illness—whether it was predominantly nervous or physical—it marked the breaking point of the tension that preceded her decision to become a nun and continued through the year of her novitiate. 'Everything was such a strain to me,' she writes, 'that if the Lord had not helped me no reflections of my own could have kept me true to my purpose.' Her nerves were pent up. Her physique, too, was ill-adjusted to the convent life. The change of food, she says, and in her way of living affected her health. After her profession, the tension snapped.

When the doctors in Ávila made her no better, Don Alonso took her to Becedas, a mountain village beyond Castellanos de la Cañada, to be treated by a *curandera*—a woman, that is to say, professing to be a healer. The result was deplorable. The treatment was so drastic that the pain, instead of being alleviated, became worse; it was as though sharp teeth were gripping hold of her. As if this were not enough, in consequence of continuous fever and purges given daily for a month, she became so shrivelled that her nerves, she says, began to shrink.

It would be wrong, however, to think of Teresa at this time as a person with her thoughts centred on her ailments. The episode of the priest at Becedas shows that this was not so. This man, who was of good family, unusually intelligent and of some learning (learning always attracted her) became very fond of her: *él se aficionó en extremo a mí*. Because of his affection, he confided in her, telling her that for nearly seven years he had been infatuated by a woman of that place; he had continued to say Mass, but his good name was gone. Possibly the woman was a gypsy, for the priest appears to have believed that she had cast a spell on him, and at her request he was wearing a copper image round his neck. At any rate Teresa, far from condemning him, showed him the greater affection 'Comencé,' she writes, 'a mostrarle más amor.' So, to please her, he gave her the image, which she handed to someone else to throw into the river. Soon after, he ended the association with the woman—for he had become like one awakening from a deep sleep. Within a year he died, devoutly and wholly freed from the infatuation: *muy bien y muy quitado de aquella ocasión.*

The episode is of interest from several angles. It is an example of Teresa's power to make others fall in with her wishes. When she was a small child, she had made her brother, Rodrigo, set out with her for the land of the Moors. When she left home for the Incarnation, she persuaded another brother, Antonio, not merely to accompany her, but to go on himself to the monastery of Santo Tomás to become a friar. In fact he was unsuited, and soon came out. Her capacity for getting her own way would be frightening were it not that she learned to put it to good use. She made mistakes, as the incident concerning Antonio shows. Towards the end of her life she made a more serious one, when she was over-zealous in encouraging a partnership between

Jerónimo Gracián and Nicolás Doria, two men diametrically opposed to each other in temperament. Yet, her mistakes of this kind were few.

She knew what she wanted, and usually got it, but she was not the domineering woman, who—particularly in England and America, where a superior manner is frequently mistaken for genuine superiority of intellect or character—rises too often, to the detriment of others, to a position of authority; becomes a hospital matron, a headmistress, a 'big business' woman or possibly a reverend mother. Teresa was not moved by personal ambition. As time went on, her strength of will was put more and more to the service of others; her energies channelled into a consuming desire to be 'the servant of love', and in this service to put right, as far as in her lay, what she believed to be at fault. This was the driving force behind the foundation of Saint Joseph's and the Reform as a whole. She did not ride rough-shod over others, but reached her goal through discretion and, above all, patience:

> La paciencia
> Todo lo alcanza.

It is true that Teresa, as she admits herself, could be 'terrible' to those whom she loved, by which she means that she found it hard to endure in them the smallest imperfection. It might, indeed, be argued that her worst fault in relation to others was a too great desire for perfection. Yet it would be wrong to think of her as someone who imposes her will, nagging and fussing about this trifle and that. What is remarkable—the more so in view of her century and background—is her tolerance, of which there is plentiful evidence if only in the reiterated re-minders to her nuns to bear with others, whether in the convent or outside it—to remember that God does not lead all by the same road. I do not pretend to like the scolding letter that she wrote to Ana de Jesús—one of her best-loved daughters—when the latter was Prioress of Granada. But at that time Teresa was old and ill and badgered with anxieties concerning the Reform. At the root of this letter is a fear (fully justified) as to what would happen if Prioresses were to make a habit of acting on their own, without regard for the Rule, or consultation with their Superiors. She knew from experience how nuns could suffer through the vagaries of such persons. In the *Foundations* she gives an instance of a Prioress who, whenever the mood took her, used to 'discipline' the nuns by making them recite the seven penitential psalms—and more besides. That, Teresa goes on, is what happens when a Superior gets above herself: 'she keeps the entire community saying prayers . . . when it would be better for them to go to sleep.' It has also to be borne in mind that the now much revered Ana de Jesús had an imperious streak in her character. The fact that she was a Carmelite nun did not prevent her from being affronted when Gracián made the mistake of addressing her as 'President' instead of 'Prioress'.

The Becedas story is an instance, too, of Teresa's compassion —and her courage. One can visualize what could have been the reaction of a young nun to the priest's story—the hasty withdrawal, the perfunctory prayers murmured by way of charity. Teresa was still young and she had her faults, but she was too large of heart for that. *Dedit ei Dominus . . . latitudinem cordis, quasi arena quae est in litore maris.* God gave her a heart, as the liturgy has put it, as boundless as the sand that is upon the sea-shore. And so she showed the greater affection.

True to her character, Teresa, as she looks back, reproaches herself over the episode of the priest, just as on another occasion she accuses herself of having too much affection for her sister. I do not believe that these reproaches go very deep. Possibly they are her instinctive answer to the reader who will say, 'What sort of a nun is this?' By admitting herself to have been at fault she silences criticism. Actions are more telling than words. Teresa may blame herself for lack of detachment, but at no period of her life does she appear, for all her strength of will, to have made an effort to cut herself off from affection for either relatives or friends. To have done so would, in her eyes, have been a withdrawal from charity. She was not the kind of nun who, in enclosing herself within convent walls, shuts out humanity. Her letters are filled with expressions of solicitude, affection, love. What she did do was to lift affection and love above the reach of possessiveness and pettiness. It was her way to serve those she loved, not to make demands on them.

*   *   *

When the *curandera's* treatment did no good, Don Alonso took Teresa home, only to be told by the doctors in Ávila that his daughter was consumptive. Then in August 1539, just before the feast of the Assumption, she had a fit which left her unconscious for four days. The *Viaticum* was brought to her, and people stood round her bed reciting the Creed—as though, she remarks dryly, she were in a state to take it in. A grave was dug in the grounds of the Incarnation, and nuns came to Don Alonso's house to watch round the corpse. She would have been buried, had not her father insisted that there was still life in her. When she returned to consciousness, she found blobs of wax on her eyelids from the funeral candles.

She was alive, but that was all. Her bones felt as if they were out of joint, there was confusion in her head, her tongue was bitten to pieces and her throat so swollen that she could not bear even to drink water. She lay rolled in a ball unable to stir hand or foot, so racked with pain that if anyone touched her it was agony. She had to be moved in a sheet lifted either end.

In this condition, she asked to be taken back to the Incarnation where the nuns, who had been expecting a corpse, welcomed her with joy. After eight months she began to go about on her hands and knees. In all, she was ill for three years.

*   *   *

Sin is Behovely, but
All shall be well, and
All manner of thing shall be well.

From the porch of the Incarnation a flight of stone steps goes up a dark *locutorio* where, behind a grille, there are relics that include a jug belonging to Teresa, a piece of her embroidery, the key of her cell and a crucifix that she took with her on her travels. There is also the drawing by Saint John of the Cross which was the inspiration for Salvador Dali's painting, *El Cristo*. The little faded pen-and-ink sketch, portraying the crucified Christ seen from the side and below the level of the observer—the head sunk on to the chest, the hair falling forward, the knees bent beneath the weight of the body—is enclosed in the simple reliquary of gilded wood into which it was placed by Doña María Pinel, Prioress of the Incarnation, to whom it was bequeathed by Ana de Jesús, the latter having received it from the saint himself.

An old portress shows these relics to visitors. She tells them, too, that in this room Teresa spoke with Peter of Alcántara and with Francis Borgia, previously Duke of Gandía, who, after serving in the army of Charles V, renounced his titles and estates to join the Society of Jesus. Below this *locutorio* she shows another—the one where Teresa's niece, Beatriz de Cepeda y Ocampo, found her aunt and Saint John of the Cross raised a couple of feet above the ground in a rapture. 'You can't speak about God to John of the Cross,' Teresa is reputed to have said, 'because he goes into an ecstasy and makes others do the same.' This lower *locutorio* opens into another, then into a third. In the last, built when Teresa was Prioress, the wooden frame enclosing the grille is modern, because visitors through the ages chipped away the wood of the original one to keep as relics. The portress explains all this, but she does not explain the real significance of these parlours in the life of Teresa. It was in the *locutorios* of the Incarnation, not in the silence of her cell, that she fought a battle in which she came near to defeat.

There was in Teresa an innate honesty—more than that, a passion for truth—that she had inherited from Don Alonso. Falsehood and insincerity were the faults that she found hardest to forgive whether in others or herself. Writing of the period following her illness she tells how, having given her father the impression of being versed in matters of prayer, even to the extent of instructing himself and others, she later found it necessary, rather than deceive him, to admit that she had ceased to pray. Then, realizing that he was puzzled and not wanting to cause him distress, she tried to cover what she had said by attributing her own state to ill-health. Don Alonso, she says, because he never told a lie himself and his relationship with his daughter was such that she had no need to lie, believed her. 'But I well knew,' she goes on, 'that I had no such excuse really.'

She makes clear in what sense she uses the word prayer. 'I could not,' she writes, 'shut myself up within myself, in which consisted my whole way of prayer.' To pray (she stresses this repeatedly) is to withdraw into oneself, like the tortoise or the hedgehog. It is to find God hidden in the innermost part of the soul, like the succulent kernel concealed among layers of leaves in the middle of the *palmito* or dwarf palm. She develops this idea in the *Interior Castle*, in which she writes of God as a King whose council chamber is in the centre of the palace. This conception of prayer first came to her as she read the *Third Spiritual Alphabet* of Francisco de Osuna which was given her by her uncle Don Pedro de Cepeda when she visited him on her way to Becedas to be treated by the *curandera*. Her copy of this book may be seen in the sacristy of Saint Joseph's convent, Ávila, along with a drum and pipes that she used to play at recreation; also one of her letters that has been decorated with bright, painted birds. It is a small volume, much scored, with yellowed leaves and heavy type. In the margins, to draw attention to passages of importance, there are signs that include a heart, a cross and a pointing hand. I had reason to remember this book

when, as I was travelling one day from Granada to Seville,
the bus drew up in a street of dazzlingly white houses. It was
Osuna, where the author of the *Third Spiritual Alphabet* was
born. White walls and iron balconies came up to the windows
of the bus. Ahead I saw more white walls and golden pantile
roofs, and overhead the glaring blue of the sky. Francisco de
Osuna, who like Ignatius Loyola was a soldier as well as a mystic, was at Tripoli when the Spaniards took the town in 1510.
He writes of prayer in the language of human love, which he
describes as 'a ladder by which the feet of the wise mount to
God'. Prayer is nothing else than a conversation, as Teresa was
later to put it, between two persons who love each other.
Moreover to love God is within the scope of all, for it is depen-
dent not on activity but on the will. 'All', he writes, 'cannot
fast or wear rough clothing, labour or journey. But if you say
you cannot love, I do not believe you.'

What she learnt from the *Third Spiritual Alphabet* she began
with characteristic impetuosity to pass on to those about her—
not only her father, who came to see her regularly at the Incarnation, but others as well. Having charm and intelligence and
the gift of inspiring confidence ('People have a blind faith in
me, I don't know why,' she says in one of her letters) she was
much sought after by visitors to the *locutorio*. Her superiors
encouraged this, since the more numerous the visitors the
more numerous, too, were the gifts to help out the meagre
resources of the community. As well as passing on the ideas
that she found in the *Third Spiritual Alphabet* she used to lend
books and explain how to make a meditation. She says that in
those days before she knew how to look after herself, she was,
as are many beginners, much occupied in trying to improve
others.

So, under the veneer of spiritual guidance, she was drawn
more and more into the shallow, gossipy world of the *locutorio*,
where her vanity was flattered and hours were frittered away.
Worse than that, she had become the slave of purposeless

emotional attachments, with the consequence that she who had presumed to teach others could no longer pray herself, no longer withdraw into the quiet of her soul. It was not merely that her mind was distracted; in the *Way of Perfection* she makes it clear that the soul can be withdrawn and at peace even when the imagination is rushing madly hither and thither. It was her guilty conscience that made prayer impossible. To pray seemed hypocrisy—as though she were setting herself up as better than others, when, if anything, she was worse. The most she could do was to say the prayers in choir that were obligatory upon the community. Even then she found herself waiting for the clock to strike.

It was strangely moving in the *locutorios* of the Incarnation with their blackened, timbered ceilings and red-tiled floors and the sunlight filtering through the high barred windows, to reflect on what Teresa describes as these wasted years of life during which she wanted, as she puts it, to reconcile things utterly opposed; the life of the spirit and the pleasures and joys and pastimes of the senses. 'Into so many and such grave occasions of sin did I fall,' she writes, 'and so far was my soul led astray by these vanities that I was ashamed to return to God and to approach him in the intimate friendship that comes with prayer.' False humility had made her afraid to pray. This was no passing phase. For nearly twenty years she was tossed on a stormy sea.

Her words, even allowing for her habitual self-reproach, are strong. Teresa was not a sinner on the scale of the Magdalen or Augustine. Nevertheless, she was vain, inconsequent—caught, too, in the mesh of those very affections which, as she well knew, were at the root of the corruption in the religious houses of her day.

The saints seem at times to be hardly more than solemn names to adorn a calendar or head the page of a missal. One is tempted to turn away feeling that with such as these one has no common ground. The classical dramatists were wise to give to their hero or heroine some flaw of character, that the audience, seeing persons of such stature to have failings like their own, might be moved to sympathy. But failings can do more than rouse compassion. It is the glorious paradox of Christianity that, through the mystery of providence, even grave sins can be made to serve God's will. On Good Friday the Church can cry:

dulce lignum, dulces clavos.

So Teresa, looking back, saw this period of her life as a cause for greater thankfulness, greater love. In spite of herself, the Hunter, *el dulce Cazador*, had overtaken her, the Good Shepherd sought her out. Those were the lean years that made more wonderful the years that followed. The poison tasted in advance by the seller of antidotes (to prove its efficacy) is the drug that heals. Her faults have given a particular character to her sanctity. Because she was vain, at the mercy of her emotions, a prey to foolish friendships; because, when she should have been praying, she was wishing the clock around, there is in Teresa's sanctity a great tolerance and humanity. Like the wind that sweeps the plain of Castile, she sweeps through not only the fustiness of her own century, but all fusty, scowling, timorous pietism that makes a mockery of the Church of Christ.

*　　　*　　　*

One evening I visited a citizen of Ávila who lived in an ancient palace adjoining the battlements. I was sitting in the *patio*, when I noticed a creature that might have been a toad, or possibly a salamander (I could not see in the half-light) moving purposefully across the flag-stones. I remembered Teresa's description of a 'something like a great toad, only crawling much more quickly' that she saw to her consternation coming towards her one day in the *locutorio* when she was gossiping with someone for whom she had much affection, who caused her much distraction—whether a man or woman the Spanish does not reveal. In her times the toad was a symbol of evil. In the Capilla Real at Granada there is a sixteenth-century Flemish painting in which the devil is represented with the face of a toad. It is not surprising then, that, overwrought as she was and her conscience troubling her, she saw in this natural happening a manifestation of the devil—a warning permitted by God's mercy.

There had been other warnings.

An elderly nun, a relative, who had been many years in the Incarnation, ventured to give her advice. Teresa was resentful; she told herself that the old woman was shocked without cause.

Another time, she says, Christ revealed himself to her with an expression of displeasure, *con mucho rigor*, making it plain that her friendships were not pleasing to him. She tried to put this from her mind, to believe it was imagination; but so vivid was the impression made upon her that it was still with her after twenty-six years. This is the first mention in her writings of anything in the nature of a vision. She did not see Christ, she says, with the eyes of the body, but, far more clearly, with those of the soul.

Don Alonso's death, in the winter of 1543, also made a deep impression on her. She went home from the Incarnation to nurse him, hoping that she was making a small return for all that he had done for her, not only at the time of her illness but throughout her life. He was always, she says, her support and comfort. Now that he was being taken from her, it was as though her soul were being torn from her body. Yet Teresa, who shed tears so easily, did not shed them now. Not to cause her father distress, she hid her grief, behaving as if she felt none; forcing herself into activity. He died on Christmas Eve 'like an angel', reminding those about him that 'all things pass'.

*   *   *

There is an *Ecce Homo* in one of the oratories at the Incarnation. The head is crowned with thorns, the eyes anguished, the lips parted. There is blood on the chest and shoulders. The hands are fastened with a rope. When I think of it, I recall the words of the psalmist: *Popule meus, quid feci tibi? Aut in quo contristavi te?* At the time it did not make a great impression on me: I had seen many of its kind in the churches of Spain. Now, I seem to see it looking at me down the dark tunnel of the centuries that separate Teresa's day from mine.

She, too, saw it in the oratory, probably in the year 1556. It was not, as now, set in a place of honour, but left on one side to be used at some festival. The fact that it was forgotten and uncared for gave it, in Teresa's eyes, a particular pathos. Moved, she says, with compassion and a sense of her own unworthiness, she fell on her knees, begging that she might have the strength to offend God no more.

A change of direction in the spiritual life (what is described by the rather unfortunate word, conversion) can be sudden. As I have said earlier, Saint Paul's conversion would appear to have been of this kind—though we do not know what searchings of heart may have preceded the vision on the road to Damascus. Usually, however, it is something that happens gradually—that, seen in retrospect, may be associated with a particular occasion, the latter being in fact the culmination or the symbol of much that has gone before. It has indeed something in common with what we call 'falling in love'.

So Teresa as she looks back sees that day in the oratory as marking a change in the direction of her life: she remembers that from then she went forward, struggling still and often falling, but with her trust now wholly in God and her purpose clear—to mould her will to his.

*   *   *

During what she remembered afterwards as wasted years of her life, God, Teresa says, chastised her with favours. By the word favour she means sometimes a vivid awareness of God's

presence. At other times she is referring to mystical phenomena, such as voices or visions.

In 1559, when as a result of an index being published by the
Grand Inquisitor some of her favourite books were removed,
she heard Christ say to her: 'Do not be dismayed. I will give
you a living book.' Similarly, when she ended her friendships
of the *locutorio*, she was comforted by hearing in the depths of
her spirit the words: 'I will have you converse not with men
but with angels.'

Another time, when she was at Mass on the feast of Saint
Paul, she saw Christ in his resurrected body in great beauty
and majesty. She nearly always saw him in the glory of his
resurrection; *con carne glorificada*. Occasionally he was wearing
a crown of thorns or was carrying his cross, but even then in his
glorified body. He used to reveal himself to her gradually.
One time he showed her the shining beauty of his hands. She
could not, however, see the colour of his eyes, or his height; if
she tried to see more than was granted to her, she lost the vision
altogether. One day he took from her hand the cross belonging
to her rosary. When he gave it back it had become four stones
more precious than diamonds, on which were the marks of the
five wounds. From that day the cross always looked like this to
her: she could no longer see the wood of which it was made.
But it was only to herself that it appeared so—to everyone else
it was as before.

Then there was the angel. He was 'not tall—on the contrary,
short, but of great beauty and his face afire.' He carried a spear
of gold with an iron tip and coming from this a flame. He
pierced her heart with this spear, several times, causing her pain
of such intensity that she moaned aloud, yet of such sweetness
that no one could have wished to forgo it. There is a Carmelite
tradition that this happened again when Teresa was Prioress.
Of all her visions it is the one that has acquired the most notor-
iety. In 1726 Benedict IX instituted the feast of the Transver-
beration of the Heart of Saint Teresa, to be observed by the

Discalced Carmelites. Later it was extended to the whole of Spain. The institution of the feast is understandable and is characteristic of the trend of eighteenth-century piety. It is another matter, however, to assert, as some have done, that the fissure visible in her heart preserved at Alba de Tormes was made by the angel's spear. Such tales do nothing to further the cause of the saints. In any case, writing in the *Spiritual Relations* of the soul being wounded like a heart pierced by an arrow, Teresa is careful to add that there is no wound in the physical sense.

Fray Pedro Ibáñez, the Dominican, remarked after reading the *Life* that the only fault he had to find was that there was so much in it about visions and revelations. Mysticism has of course its place in the Church, yet the attitude of the Church is guarded. It is well represented in the words of a certain Fray Juan Hurtado who, when confronted with an apparition as he was praying declared: 'I do not want this favour to be granted to me, for I believe firmly enough without the help of any such wonders.' In the sifting of evidence for canonization, visions and such manifestations are suspect, nor are they ever accepted as a substitute for the practice of the virtues. There are many saints who never saw a vision. Equally, visionaries are not necessarily saints; if they were, as Saint Boniface remarked, Balaam and his ass would both have been canonized.

Because mystics were particularly prevalent in Teresa's Spain, the attitude taken by the Church was the more uncompromising. The Inquisitors made it their business to hunt down false mystics, many of whom were women. Teresa was well aware of this. She knew, also, the penalties meted out to them in the courts of the Inquisition—and the yet worse penalties imposed by the civil courts to which the accused, if held guilty of witchcraft, were handed on. She believed that her visions came from God. Nevertheless, she was always questioning their reality, always in dread of being deluded. Much of her writing is an honest attempt to analyse her experiences, to see them dispassionately, to discriminate for her own sake and the sake of others between the false and the true—what comes from God and what from the devil; what, too, is merely imagination. She was fully alive to the possibility of auto-suggestion. Writing about two nuns to the Prioress of Seville she says: 'They would not have had such a whirl of experiences if they had been with me! The very fact that they have had so many makes me suspicious.'

But after all she was an ignorant woman. This is Teresa's reiterated lament—the ignorance of her own sex; the fact that they are without the learning which is the key to so much. Again and again she expresses her respect for learning and intelligence. 'If you want us to serve you well in these houses of ours, my Father, send us women of intelligence,' she writes to one of the Carmelites of the Reform, Mariano de San Benito, 'and you will see that we shall not be in the least worried about their dowries.' When a Prioress complained that a nun was too fond of reading, Teresa retorted: 'Better a bookworm than a fool!' She lists among the duties of a Prioress that of providing books for the community and, where necessary, teaching novices to read. She regretted that she herself had not more leisure for reading.

Lacking then, as she believed, the knowledge that was needed, she confided her spiritual experiences to persons whom she had reason to regard as better equipped than herself to form a judgement. One of these was Francisco de Salcedo, a gentleman of Ávila, a married man much given to prayer, *un caballero santo*, who used to come to see her at the Incarnation. He, in turn, introduced her to Gaspar Daza, a prebendary of the cathedral reputed for his learning. The latter gave her advice, but refused to hear her confession: he said he was too busy. He probably had no wish to run the risk of exposing himself to the odium of the Inquisitors through being associated with a woman who might prove to be a victim of hysteria. However, at the suggestion of Salcedo she wrote as best she could an account, to be read by himself and Daza, of what she had experienced in prayer. After much deliberation, they told her that, as far as they could judge, she was being deluded by Satan. It would be wise, they said, to consult a certain Juan de Prádanos, a Jesuit at the Colegio de San Gil, who would visit her at the Incarnation. She was so distressed by their verdict that she could only weep.

Juan de Prádanos (years later, in a letter to María Bautista, Teresa calls him her 'good friend') took a different view. He believed that she was being led by God. This was also the view of another Jesuit, Baltasar Álvarez, who became her confessor at this time. It was at the suggestion of the latter, who treated her with 'great gentleness', that she eventually ended the friendships of the *locutorio*. She was supported even more strongly by Peter of Alcántara, with whom she corresponded and had many conversations.

Ávila is a small place. What happens to one person can easily become the property of all. Teresa, who had spoken of her experiences to a number of people, and by no means always under the seal of confession, soon found that she was being talked about. She asked the portress at the Incarnation not to mention the visit of Juan de Prádanos. However, someone saw him arrive, with the result that the convent could talk of nothing else. It was the same in the city. It did her, she says, much harm. Things were divulged which should have been kept secret. Besides, the impression was given that she was publishing these matters abroad in a spirit of vainglory. Some persons, genuinely concerned for her, were afraid that she would be asked to appear before the Inquisition. Others were hostile. They mocked at this visionary who had appeared among them; said that she was possessed by the devil and should be exorcized. Some of her critics questioned her closely; then, because they did not like her answers, accused her of being lacking in humility; they complained that a 'mere woman' should have the effrontery to instruct them. Padre Álvarez, who was young and subject to a rigid superior, also found himself exposed to criticism. One cleric who heard her confession during Álvarez's absence was especially insistent that Teresa was the victim of Satan, after which she was told not merely to make the sign of the cross when she saw a vision, but to snap her fingers at it in derision. To avoid having continually to cross herself, she carried a cross with her. As to snapping her fingers, she decided not to be too particular about obeying this order.

* * *

Teresa's mystical experiences, as well as her whole conception of the spiritual life, have come down to us in her writings. In these one can trace the influence of Francisco de Osuna, Saint Jerome, Saint Gregory, Saint Augustine, and, above all, of the Scriptures from which she quotes freely, if not always accurately. Another influence, less obvious but not less forcible, is that of the romantic tales of chivalry which had so gripped her imagination as a girl that, according to Ribera, she and her brother had themselves written one. 'She had so excellent a wit,' her biographer says, 'and had so well absorbed the language and the style of chivalry that in the space of a few months she and her brother Rodrigo composed a book of adventure and fictions on that subject, which was such that it attracted a great deal of comment.' Time and again she presents the spiritual life in terms of an adventure in which the soul, fired with love, dares all for Love. Indeed, her imagery is often more suggestive of the passionate love symbolized by *Eros* than of the Christian *Agape*. Had this been pointed out to her, she would have replied, I imagine, that the distinction between the two is not always easy to draw.

It was not, however, her reading that taught Teresa how to write, but her natural wit. Her lively mind was packed with ideas jostling one another to find expression. 'I only wish,' she says, 'that I had two hands to write with, so as not to forget one thing while I am saying another.' Her powers of observation were enormous. She gives expression to her ideas in images picked at random from the world that she sees round her. Grace is a shining river, sin a sluggish pool. A bad habit is as hard to uproot as a plant that, having been watered every day, has grown so strong that it has to be dug out with a spade. A soul full of eager desires is like a fountain spurting up from the earth; a soul in rapture like vapour drawn heavenward by the sun. A soul that has not recourse to God moves at the pace of a hen. Persons who occupy themselves with unessentials are compared to a little shepherd boy, *pastorcillo*, who finding himself in the presence of the King can only gaze dumbfounded at the splendour of the royal robes. Someone at the mercy of a stupid director is as frustrated as a tethered gosling. Those who live by prayer are as safe as the spectators who watch a bull-fight from the grandstand. The very richness of Teresa's writing sometimes gives an appearance of confusion. She mixes metaphors, goes off at a tangent. Yet it would be wrong to conclude that her thought lacks clarity. She describes her mystical experiences with a discernment and exactness the more remarkable coming from one who by academic standards was scarcely educated.

Writing of locutions she explains that the voices she heard were audible not to the ears of the body but those of the soul. Only twice did she hear voices with her bodily ears, and neither time were they distinct. The voices she heard in the soul, on the other hand, were startlingly clear; moreover, the words remained fixed in her mind years afterwards. Many of these locutions took the form of expressions of encouragement or reassurance—as, for example, when Christ spoke to her before the founding of Saint Joseph's. She heard him, too, at Toledo, when she was doubtful whether to go to Pastrana at the request of the Princess of Éboli. It is noticeable that the voices became fewer as the need for them grew less—as her confidence became greater and her tasks were accomplished. Yet they did not cease. In the last winter of her life, when she wondered if she could face the journey from Ávila to Burgos, she heard Christ speaking to her, giving her the necessary courage.

Her visions, too, though they continued, became less frequent. Especially those that she describes as imaginary. She does not mean by this that they were illusions, mere figments of the imagination. She is using the word in the technical sense, as employed by mystical theologians, to denote a vision that presents itself to the soul in the form of a picture or *imago* and can therefore, metaphorically speaking, be said to be visible to the eyes of the soul as distinct from those of the body. She says in the *Spiritual Relations* that she did not at any time see corporal visions—that is, visions apprehended by bodily eyes. At first, this worried her: she concluded that anything seen otherwise than by the eyes of the body must of necessity be a delusion. Later, she came to believe that the chance of delusion was less in the case of imaginary than corporal visions, and least of all when the visions were intellectual or apprehended by the soul without the medium of a pictorial representation of any kind. Though certain of the reality of the intellectual vision, she had the greatest difficulty in explaining this in words. It was something clothed in darkness; an abstraction that made its impact in the secret places of the soul. How did she know, her bewildered confessor asked her, that Christ was at her side, if she could neither see him nor hear him nor was there anyone to tell her it was he? She could only reply that she knew it with a certainty greater than any that can come through the senses. It was like knowing, in the dark, that someone is beside you—yet the comparison, she admitted, was inadequate.

If the purpose of the locutions was to give encouragement and reassurance, that of the visions seems to have been to strengthen her belief in the doctrines of the Church. While it is true that Teresa accepted the Catholic faith unquestioningly, she did not believe without thinking. She brought her intelligence to bear on her beliefs to a degree that is the more astonishing in one whose mind was untrained; who lived, moreover, in an age when for a woman to think was looked upon with ill-favour. Her mind dwells constantly on the mystery of the Trinity and its implications. The three persons are distinct, she reflects, yet are one in will, essence, dominion and Godhead. 'Could the Son create an ant without the Father? No, for their power is all one. And the same is true of the Holy Spirit, so that there is one almighty God and three persons comprising one majesty. Could we love the Father without loving the Son and the Holy Spirit too? No, for whoever pleases one of these three divine persons pleases all three; and equally so with whoever offends them. Could the Father exist without the Son and without the Holy Spirit? No, for there is one essence, and where the one is there are all the three, for they are indivisible. How is it then that we see the three persons divided, and how came it that the Son took human flesh and not the Father nor the Holy Spirit?' In the *Interior Castle* she shows how, in the Seventh Mansion, the soul not only believes the truth of the Trinity but apprehends it as though in a flash of lightning clarity. Commenting in the *Spiritual Relations* on a vision of the Trinity, she says that what is revealed is indeed above human understanding, yet the benefit to the soul from such a revelation surpasses all that can be derived from years of meditation.

The mystic is like a traveller who has returned from a land so unlike his own, so strange and wonderful, that he has no words in which to tell of it. He tries to speak but the language, put to a use beyond its powers, falters and breaks beneath the strain. Time has no words for things eternal, nor earth for heaven. Lazarus, brought back from the dead, was silent.

When Teresa tried to put into words a vision of the glorified Christ, she felt as if her whole being were disrupted. In the *Interior Castle* she says that she can no more describe the wonders she has seen than she can the countless treasures that were shown her, one day, in the castle of the Duke of Alba. At a loss, she turns to the imagery of light. The Godhead is a bright cloud or a glittering diamond. Christ and the Virgin are clothed in light. The Holy Spirit is a dove that flutters above her head 'for the space of an *Ave Maria*' on wings made of tiny shells of great brilliance. As in the *Paradiso*, all is light. Sometimes her mind turns to pictures with which she is familiar. She was very fond of pictures. The memory of the painting of the Samaritan woman at the well was with her all her life. At the Incarnation she decorated her oratory with pictures. She had pictures painted for the hermitages at Saint Joseph's. At Toledo she spent the little money she possessed on two paintings to go behind the altar. In the church belonging to the friars at Duruelo she was delighted by a rough drawing of Christ, almost certainly done by Saint John of the Cross, which was fastened above the holy water stoup. She mentions there being at Mancera, four miles from Duruelo, a Flemish picture of the Virgin owned by Don Luis, Lord of the Five Towns, who had built a church to house it. She saw a vision of the risen Christ as she had seen him in paintings. The suffering Christ appeared to her 'as he is painted in the *Sixth Anguish*'. On the eve of Saint Sebastian, just as the *Salve Regina* was beginning in the choir of the Incarnation, she saw the Virgin with a multitude of angels (they were above the misericords and on the kneeling rests of the stalls), as she was painted in a picture given her by the Countess of Osorno.

She describes what it is like to go into a rapture. Until she became used to it, it was an alarming experience: enough to make the hair stand on end. Without warning she felt as though she were being carried up on the wings of a powerful eagle. To resist was as useless as to fight against a giant. Sometimes, in a state of rapture, the soul, she says, experiences a strange, yet delectable loneliness, as if it were perched on a roof-top above created things. *Vigilavi et factus sum sicut passer solitarius in tecto.* At other times, it suffers an acute restlessness; seems to wander from place to place, saying to itself, 'Where is my God?'

She says, too, that the soul seems to draw the body after it. She is speaking metaphorically. Yet there were times when this happened actually. Teresa did not soar high into the air like Peter of Alcántara who, if we are to believe one of the witnesses giving evidence for his canonization, flew up to the tops of trees, uttering a weird shriek which terrified his brethren: *edebat clamores adeo terrificos et terribiles ut horrore percuterentur fratres.* She did, however, leave the ground. Once when there were grand ladies in the chapel for a patronal festival, she had to get the nuns to hold her down: she was 'worn out with the worry of it all'. Another time Ana de la Encarnación, a nun at the Segovia convent, found her between one and two o'clock in the afternoon kneeling in the choir about half a yard above the floor. Bishop Diego de Yepes, her biographer, who knew her well, relates that one day, when she felt a rapture coming upon her, she caught hold of some mats in an effort to keep herself down and rose into the air with these still in her hands. Another day, he says, she rose above the level of the *comulgatorio* (the opening in the wall of the choir through which the nuns received Holy Communion) so that it was not possible for him to give her the Host. However these experiences are to be explained, they caused Teresa acute embarrassment. Writing about raptures to her brother Lorenzo she says: 'Several times I have had them in public—during Matins, for example. It is useless to resist them and they are impossible to conceal. I get so dreadfully ashamed that I feel I want to hide away somewhere. I pray God earnestly not to let them happen to me in public; will you make this prayer for me too, for it is an extremely awkward thing and I don't believe my prayer is any the better for it.'

Luis de León, who was as sceptical where visions were concerned as Pedro Ibáñez, wrote to Ana de Jesús in 1588 that the genuineness of Teresa's revelations was borne out by the good effects they had both on herself and the whole of her Order. In his opinion, they could be regarded as a touchstone by which similar manifestations might be judged. His attitude is a reasonable one, in line with the words of Christ: 'By their fruit ye shall know them.' It is, moreover, the attitude taken by the Church today regarding the apparitions, for example, at Fatima: whether or not the details given by the children and other witnesses are objectively true, the effects produced in the Church by the apparitions have proved to be good.

Teresa's visions and locutions confirmed her soul in tranquillity and resoluteness of purpose. They were a source of inspiration and encouragement. She says that they gave her fortitude; that without their help she could not have put up with the incalculable amount of trouble, opposition and ill-health that she had to endure. On one occasion, when neither her confessors nor men of learning could calm her, she found peace in the simple words heard in the depth of her soul: 'It is I. Be not afraid.'

She emphasized the importance of this spiritual calm in regard to mystical phenomena in general. Those that are divine, she says, bring peace, making the recipient better equipped to serve God in the world. On the other hand, manifestations that are from the devil are, like the devil himself, productive of discontent, restlessness, scruples, and false humility. The soul that is deluded by Satan is, besides, vainglorious; attributing to spiritual favours an importance they do not possess, forgetting these are no proof of sanctity nor even of goodness. The soul that is humble neither desires such experiences nor asks for them; nor, when they come, does it try to prolong them. Teresa, far from asking for revelations, prayed, and asked others to pray, that she might be led another way.

To say that her revelations are genuine is not necessarily to maintain that each vision was sent, directly, by God, like a picture flashed upon a screen. For the Christian all good gifts come down from the Father of Light. Whether they come directly or through the intermediary channels of nature matters little. Background, environment, temperament—these, and whatever other influences go to make the personality, have their part in the making of the saint. Grace does not change nature, but works upon it and perfects it.

*   *   *

The devil appears to have had a free hand in Castile; though, if we are to believe Teresa, he had yet more scope in Andalusia. She saw him many times during her years at the Incarnation. Once, on the night of All Souls, he sat on her breviary just as she had finished saying a nocturn. Another time he appeared to her in one of the oratories 'in an abominable form'. A great flame, which was 'intensely bright and casting no shadow', was coming out of his body. He also appeared in the shape of a hideous blackamoor, gnashing his teeth. Sometimes he pummelled her and even tried to strangle her, which, apart from being unpleasant, was embarrassing, since the other nuns, to whom he was not visible, wondered what was happening. When he went away, he left a smell of brimstone behind him. One Trinity Sunday she saw a host of devils fighting against angels. Another day, at a funeral, a number of devils were dragging the body about and pulling the shroud with great hooks. In the Carmelite convent in Granada I was shown a little wooden cross enclosed now in silver, which Teresa used to carry with her to frighten the devil. The sign of the cross was an effective weapon. But a sprinkling of holy water was even more so. 'Keep some holy water near you,' she writes to her brother Lorenzo, 'for there is nothing that puts an evil spirit to flight so effectively.... But the spirit will not flee unless the holy water touches it, so you must sprinkle it all around.'

When Teresa writes that she saw the devil, she does not mean with bodily eyes, but, as in the case of her heavenly visions, with those of the soul. As far as her reader is concerned, the distinction makes little difference. Nor does it matter if the devils that appeared to her had an objective reality or were the product of her own unresolved conflicts and preoccupation with guilt. Whatever their source they were real to her—

enemies to contend with. She did, in fact, contend with them so successfully that as time went on she was able to laugh at them—to care no more about them than if they had been so many flies. Moreover, the sight of a devil could be turned to a positive end. So one day during Mass, when she saw two of them with their horns gripping the throat of the celebrant, she was granted a deeper realization of the truth that the sinfulness of a priest does not invalidate the Sacrament.

So much, then, for the devil (or devils) that Teresa saw or thought she saw—in short, a mediaeval devil such as she would have expected to see. Today no doubt he would have taken a different form. I can think, for example, of a clairvoyant who claims to have seen the devil in a public house in Fulham, looking like any other of the customers—yet the devil, unmistakably, nevertheless.

More important in Teresa's teaching, because more formidable, is the unseen devil of whose activities she is always conscious; the personification and source of all evil both in the world at large and in her own life; the 'father of lies', 'lurking wherever there is darkness enough to hide him', waiting to ensnare the soul at every step of its journey. In the *Interior Castle* she represents him as being at the door of each room ready to bar the way—for this purpose he will muster whole legions of evil spirits—and the further advanced the soul, the more violent are their onslaughts.

His methods are those of subtlety and deception. He is a 'skilful painter', able to conjure up false visions and in the twinkling of an eye take on the semblance of an angel of light. Above all, he is persistent, working ceaselessly 'like a noiseless file' as he turns truth into falsehood, falsehood into truth. Some souls he casts down in a travesty of humility, causing them to be abject, diffident, slaves to scruples, incapable, so they believe, of any good action, afraid to pray, thinking of God 'as one who is always wielding fire and sword'. Others he puffs up with pride, making them suppose that they have virtues which they do not possess: to achieve this 'he will run a thousand times round hell'. Her searching analysis of the devil's handiwork caused a psychologist to remark to me that Teresa, in the sphere of the spiritual life, anticipated Alfred Adler in her understanding of the many manifestations of false humility and pride, conditions seemingly the antithesis of each other yet stemming from the same source—in Teresa's view from the devil, in Adler's from a deep sense of inferiority. Whatever the nature of the devil's attack she shows him as being before all else the enemy of tranquillity. She says that he bandies the soul about as though playing ball with it: *como jugando a la pelota con el alma;* making it restless, discontented, feckless. Worst of all, working in certain cases on the emotions, nerves and imagination or taking advantage of some physical debility, he implants a deep imprisoning melancholy that can be the beginning of despair.

This devil—not the demon breathing fire or the snarling negro—is the enemy that gives Teresa cause to fear. Yet the word fear can be misleading. She had little patience with those who spread despondency—persons who were for ever saying 'the devil this' and 'the devil that', when they could have been talking of God. 'I am more afraid,' she writes, 'of those who are terrified of the devil than I am of the devil himself.' In her view he is not so much to be feared as to be fought. Nor among the weapons to be used against him is common sense to be despised. She tells her friend, Don Teutonio de Braganza, that when he feels 'oppressed' he should go to some place where he can 'see the sky and take a walk'. 'Our nature,' she adds, 'must not be subjected to undue constraint.' Similarly in regard to the religious, Superiors should see to it that those inflicted with melancholia are not allowed to pray for long stretches of time nor be much alone, 'in case they imagine things'; nor should excessive demands be made upon them, causing them to commit sins which they cannot avoid committing. Above all, in this warfare against Satan courage is called for. If God gives courage, the adversary can do little: he will soon be in flight, 'clapping his hands to his head.'

If the devil was real to Teresa, so was hell. She saw it depicted in all the terror of mediaeval imagery in the paintings of Hieronymus Bosch and those of his school that hung upon the walls of palaces, convents and churches. She saw it on *retablos* and diptychs, carvings and stained glass. She listened to preachers thundering about flames as real as those that were being kindled by the Inquisition in Seville and Toledo and Valladolid. To borrow words used by an old Scottish laird to describe his religious upbringing, she had learnt from early childhood to 'warm' her belief in eternity 'at the furnace of hell'. It is not, then, surprising to read that one day at the Incarnation she found herself, without knowing how, 'plunged right into hell' —into a place of mud and reptiles, stench, darkness, imprisonment, where she was enclosed in 'a hollow space scooped out of a wall, like a cupboard'. All was pitchy darkness, oppression, suffocation and an agony of such a kind that the soul seemed 'to tear itself to pieces'. It was her own hell; there is no mention of other persons. It is significant that for Teresa damnation is before anything else a state of constraint, imprisonment—the negation of that 'freedom of the children of God' which characterizes her conception of what should be the relationship between the soul and its Creator. This vision remained with her all her life. Yet, unlike Saint Ignatius, in her spiritual writings she has little to say about eternal punishment. The Lord, she says, led her by the way of love.

3

The convent of Saint Joseph

IN the letter signed by the Papal Nuncio and the Bishop of Ávila, giving me the necessary permission to enter the enclosure of the Incarnation, mention of Saint Joseph's had been overlooked through a misunderstanding. In consequence, I had to visit a canon of the cathedral who, since he was seeing the Nuncio in Madrid, had offered to put this right.

Living in the same house as this canon was another, a courteous, elderly man, good-looking in a nervous horse-like way, who had written a book in which he presented, clearly tabulated, the evidence taken from the *Processes* for Teresa's canonization, as well as other documents in support of the long-standing tradition that she was born within the precincts of Ávila. In this he deals scathingly with a recent author who claims that, in fact, she was born about ten miles to the north of the city, at Gotarrendura, a village in the province of Ávila, where the Cepeda household used to pass the winter months on an estate belonging to Doña Beatriz. The crux of the matter appears to be whether or not the family would have returned to their city home by March 28th, the day of Teresa's birth, when, it must be admitted, the weather generally continues to be severe. The question is complicated by the fact that the expression *Ciudad de Ávila*, which recurs in the documents, can be applied equally to the city and the surrounding country. To an outsider the matter seems of little importance. In Ávila, however, feelings run high. The canon told me with some emotion that it would be injudicious on my part to attempt to write about the saint without making myself familiar with the contents of his book. The matter came up another day outside

Pepillo's restaurant. A lady sitting at the table with me warned me suddenly to have nothing to do with a certain Carmelite father who, she said, supported the Gotarrendura argument. 'He is no friend of Ávila,' she said hotly. 'He is trying to rob the city of its saint.'

The permit came from Madrid, but it still needed the Bishop's signature. To hasten matters I decided to visit the Bishop myself. I was in some trepidation as I went into the courtyard of the Palacio Episcopal, a shabby, dignified building of pinky cream stone adjoining the city walls near the Puerta Alcázar. In Teresa's day it was the Jesuit College, in which, at her suggestion, her nephews, the two sons of Lorenzo de Cepeda, were educated, when their father returned from the New World.

After I had repeated several times the phrase: '*Quiero ver al obispo, por favor*' ('I want to see the Bishop, please), adding: '*Es muy importante*', a blank-faced young cleric wearing iron-rimmed spectacles took me up a flight of stone stairs into a spacious room, simply furnished—its shutters closed against the sun. Presently a door opened and a small figure came in, grey-haired, wearing a magenta cassock. He looked lost in the empty, shadowy room. I dropped on one knee to kiss his ring and in halting Spanish helped out by Latin asked him that, since I was hoping to write about Saint Teresa, I might be allowed to enter the enclosure of Saint Joseph's. He answered in Spanish with elegance and such clarity that it would have been impossible to fail to understand that I had his sanction to go into both the Incarnation and Saint Joseph's as often as I pleased until my writing was finished. After receiving a blessing both for myself and my book, I departed.

Saint Joseph's is hidden by immense garden walls and the façade of a seventeenth-century chapel. In Teresa's time it had an unbroken view of the plain and the mountains. Writing in 1561 to her brother Lorenzo in America, she says that though the house is small and poor, the grounds and outlook are splendid. She was thanking him for an unexpected gift of money which, along with two dowries paid in advance and more gifts from her friend Doña Guiomar de Ulloa, had made the purchase of the house possible. Not that she had waited until she was sure of the money. She had, indeed, gone ahead with her plans (and this without telling her superiors) to the extent of arranging with her brother-in-law, Juan de Ovalle, to acquire a house in his name—this, to avoid disclosing the real purpose of the deal—and had then engaged workmen.

Inside, the building is dark and cramped. Ceilings are low, walls thick and bulging, passages twisting. The floors are on different levels, for the original house, proving too small, was enlarged by the addition of two neighbouring ones. I was shown the kitchen with its rough, soot-stained walls, where Teresa used to take her turn to cook for the community and was once, so the story goes, found in ecstasy, a saucepan in her hand. I stood, too, on the dark steep staircase known as the *Escalera del diablo*, on which on Christmas Eve 1577 she broke her arm when she fell on her way down to choir. The nuns said it was the devil's doing. Teresa's answer was cryptic; she said the devil could do worse to her than that. The following February the arm was giving her considerable pain. 'It is still swollen,' she writes in a letter to Gracián, 'and so is the hand. I am wearing a saffron plaster, which is like a coat of mail.' In May, after treatment from a *curandera*, she writes: 'I think I am better now, though the pain still tortures me so much that I cannot be sure if the cure is complete. But I can move the hand properly and raise the arm to the head.' In fact, the arm never wholly recovered its use.

Saint Joseph's is dark. Yet, at the turn of a passage there are unexpected little oratories bright with gilding and pictures and statues. The sunlight, too, breaks on the white walls of the nuns' cells, each austerely simple with a brown-covered bed and a plain wooden cross. Teresa's cell, in which she finished the writing of the *Life* and afterwards wrote the *Way of Perfection*, looks on to a *patio*, above which is a balustrade where hangs the cracked ancient bell that she brought with her from the Incarnation. In the immense overgrown garden there are four hermitages decorated in gay colours. There is also a well that, when Teresa founded the convent, gave a mere trickle of water, not fit to drink. She describes in the book of the *Foundations* how some workmen she sent for said nothing could be done; they laughed at her, telling her that she would be throwing away money. Nevertheless she persisted, with the result that soon there was plenty of fresh water. Even the Bishop condescended to drink it.

Love was the driving force behind the founding of Saint Joseph's: love and compassion. Loving Christ, the Word made Flesh, Teresa was moved to compassion at the thought that his friends were few. She writes in the *Way of Perfection*: 'Since my one desire was, and still is, that, as he has so many enemies and so few friends, these last should be faithful ones, I determined to do the little that was in my power—namely to follow the evangelical counsels as perfectly as possible.' Saint Joseph's and her subsequent foundations were Teresa's contribution to the Counter-Reformation, to a war that was being waged by the Church not only against Lutheranism, but against corruption within itself.

Today there are, one hopes, few Catholics who question the sincerity of those whom the Church calls 'Our separated brethren'. In sixteenth-century Spain an attitude of tolerance was unthinkable. To Teresa the Lutherans (she uses the term a little wildly to cover all those who in her day had cut themselves off from the primacy of Peter) are nothing else than the enemies of God, who in France and the Netherlands—wherever, indeed, they can get a footing—are destroying the churches, breaking down the images of Christ and his saints, murdering the religious, desecrating the Blessed Sacrament, spreading false doctrine. They must be fought and repelled. But there are worse enemies within the Church. 'No wonder,' she writes, 'the Church is as it is, when the religious live as they do; when those who ought to be models on which all may pattern their virtues are annulling the work done in the Orders through the spirit of the saints of old.'

Teresa was forty-three when the idea of the Reform[1] originated in a conversation that took place in the year 1558 in her cell at the Incarnation between herself and a few friends— among them her young cousin María de Cepeda y Ocampo, who was later to become Prioress at Valladolid. The suggestion was made that a convent should be founded where a few persons so disposed should live in accordance with the Primitive Rule of the Carmelite Order given by Fray Hugo, Cardinal of Santa Sabina, in the year 1248, before it was mitigated by Pope Eugenius in 1432. It was to be a simple life lived in the spirit of the ancient hermits of Mount Carmel, devoted in particular to prayer on behalf of the preachers and learned men whom in the book of the *Foundations* Teresa calls 'the champions and defenders of the Church'. It would be symbolized by the word Discalced or 'barefooted', an expression which in Carmelite history has become synonymous with Reformed, being used to designate the friars and nuns who were followers of Teresa as distinct from the Calced Carmelites who did not accept her Reform. The word has to be interpreted with some degree of latitude. Saint John of the Cross and Fray Antonio de Jesús, the first friars in the monastery that was founded at Duruelo were barefooted. At Salamanca, too, the Discalced students used to walk barefoot through streets covered with ice and snow. Teresa, however, who as she grew older allowed herself to be guided more and more by good sense, was in favour of sandals being worn. Writing in 1576 to Padre Mariano de San Benito she says it is 'really amusing' that she should be quoted as wishing the friars to go barefoot since she had herself forbidden Antonio de Jesús to do so (he was now sixty-six and in indifferent health). 'There is too much going barefoot,' she continues,

[1] See Appendix, p. 182

and points out how absurd it is in Toledo to see barefooted young friars riding on mules for distances that they could walk. As to the nuns, from the beginning they wore sandals, called *alpargatas*, with thick soles made of hemp.

Though the idea of the Reform immediately attracted Teresa she admits that in the early stages she did not consider the matter very seriously. As yet she felt no wish to leave the convent of the Incarnation; she liked the large pleasant building and her own spacious cell. Then, almost before she realized it, the plan had begun to take shape. Her cousin María de Cepeda was able to provide some money. Doña Guiomar de Ulloa offered more. They would buy a small house, they decided. It would not do on the Day of Judgment to have a huge, ornate building crashing down on thirteen nuns—for that was to be the number, signifying Christ and the Apostles. Teresa was serious now, she heard Christ speaking to her: giving her commands and making promises. He told her that the convent was to be dedicated to Saint Joseph: that he himself would keep watch at one door, the Virgin at the other: that it would give out its light, like a star: *sería una estrella que diese de sí gran resplandor.*

Somerset Maugham in *Don Fernando*, his elegant study of sixteenth-century Spain, complains that Teresa contributed to the ruin of her unhappy country by adding to the already too numerous nuns; also, that she was over-zealous in enforcing a stricter rule. He misses the point. Admittedly Teresa did add to the number of nuns, but the houses she established were of a different quality from those already in existence: they were for women who genuinely wanted to live the religious life, not a refuge for disappointed society ladies. Persons who were unsuited were not to be taken. If they were taken through an error, they were not to be kept—no matter how large a dowry they might bring. Moreover novices, she says in the *Constitutions*, must be allowed to receive visitors so that if they are discontented they have 'the chance of letting it be known that they do not wish to stay'. She did not want nuns who had come into a convent to escape the world—she had seen too many of that kind. Nor was it her intention to impose her reforms on convents other than her own. She reformed the Incarnation reluctantly, only because she was ordered to do so. The only other instance was at Alcalá de Henares, where she was called in because an autocratic Prioress was making life impossible.

The founding of Saint Joseph's comes into Teresa's story like a burst of sunlight. All at once she seems to be liberated from her past. The emotional tension is relaxed; she is no longer a victim of heart-searchings, doubts and fears. At forty-seven she has left her spiritual adolescence behind her; found the purpose of her life, scope for her gifts and an outlet for her creative energy. 'I must not be cowardly, but put all I can into this task,' she writes to Lorenzo. The difficulties that confront her are a spur to action. She has moments of discouragement, but they pass, leaving her confident and amused. She writes of this period both in the *Life* and the *Foundations* with a quiet dry humour and with that note of tranquillity that becomes increasingly evident as the years go on. If it is God's will, Saint Joseph's will be founded. If not, she would gladly forgo the founding of a hundred convents.

The plan was secret at first. Then, when it leaked out, there was turmoil. The people of Ávila laughed and jeered. In a city already packed with convents were they to be asked to contribute towards yet another? It was just the crazy idea to be expected from a woman! But their indignation arose not simply from the fact that Teresa was founding another convent— women had done that before—but because she was presuming to introduce a reform within the framework of the Order to which she belonged. The nuns at the Incarnation felt insulted. Who did she think she was? There were better than she, content to stay where they were. If she must do something, why did she not raise money for her own convent? But of course she had no love for it. Some went so far as to say that she ought to be locked up.

She was denounced from the pulpit. While she was sitting in church with her sister, the preacher began to rant about religious who left their convents to found new Orders. Juana, concerned and indignant, looked at Teresa, only to find that she was having a quiet laugh: *con gran paz se estaba riendo*. Well-intentioned persons warned her that, the times being as they were, she might find herself summoned before the Inquisition. She laughed again; if she saw any likelihood of that, she would forestall it by paying them a visit herself.

Even those in sympathy were chary of giving her public support. Padre Ibáñez approved, but kept himself, as far as possible, in the background. The Provincial of the Carmelites gave his sanction to the foundation, then withdrew it on the day before the deeds for the house were to be signed. Padre Álvarez, when she most needed her confessor's help and comfort, wrote her a scolding letter (this she found harder to bear than anything) telling her she must realize that the whole thing was a dream and should be abandoned before she gave further scandal. As though to bring the matter to a close, on Christmas Day 1561, an order came from the Provincial telling her to leave Ávila at once for Toledo, to stay with Doña Luisa de la Cerda, daughter of the Duke of Medinaceli, who was in deep distress at the death of her husband.

*   *   *

Six months later Teresa came back to Ávila.

That evening a Brief that had been applied for by Doña Guiomar de Ulloa arrived from Rome, giving the Pope's authority for founding the convent. The same evening, the Bishop of Ávila, Don Álvaro de Mendoza, visited Teresa at the Incarnation, and despite himself was won over to her cause. She was indebted for this visit to Peter of Alcántara who, ill though he was, had ridden over on a mule from his monastery at Arenas.

*   *   *

I remember the six-hour bus journey from Ávila to Arenas de San Pedro, squeezed between a priest with a blue, ill-shaven chin and a stout peasant woman carrying a squawking fowl in a basket. I was astonished when, on a lonely stretch of road in the Sierra de Gredos, the bus stopped and the passengers began bundling out. Then I saw that they were forming a queue to drink in turn from a rill that was leaping down the face of a rock. Much of this road is through country that is splendidly austere, once (perhaps still, for all I know) the haunt of brigands. It twists and climbs and dips, crosses streams and gullies. Further south the scene becomes luxuriant with olives and vines, fig trees, lemons and oranges.

Another time, when travelling this way, I broke my journey at the Fonda de Santa Teresa on the roadside among the mountains. Formerly an inn, it was at the time of my visit a holiday home for children, owned by two elderly sisters, the daughters of a doctor, with mild, well-bred faces. They entertained me in a room with a flagged floor, chairs made from withies bent into suitable shapes, and woodwork painted a bright blue. One of them spoke to me in Spanish with an occasional word of English, the other in French. They gave me sugared cakes and wine in tiny, delicately cut glasses. 'Vino de Misa,' they told me apologetically and opened a bright blue door into what seemed to be a cupboard in the wall. Inside was an altar prepared for Mass. They took me up a scrubbed wooden staircase into one room after another filled with old-fashioned iron bedsteads painted the same blue as the woodwork. Everything was spotless. Then we went down into a kitchen with pots and pans hanging on the walls, and a great cauldron suspended by a chain over a fire of pine-branches on an open hearth. An old woman in black was crouching over the fire, the light playing on her wizened face. Two little children stood with hands linked staring at me. This kitchen, the sisters told me, went back to Teresa's times. There is a tradition that she and Peter of Alcántara, when travelling in opposite directions, happened to meet at this point along the road and delayed their journey some hours while conversing with each other.

Arenas de San Pedro is in a valley with the mountains standing up all about it. Storks built on the ancient tower of its church, and a Roman bridge spans a river that, coursing over its stony bed, looks as though it were strewn with crystals. There is, too, an imposing castle, intact were it not that it has no roof. I remember the reply of a landowner living on his estate at Arenas to whom it was suggested that the castle would make an excellent hotel: '*Por pobres que seamos, nosotros no vendemos nunca nuestros castillos.*' We may be poor but we never sell our castles.

Above the town, near a plantation of sweet-scented pines, there is a Discalced convent with a spick and span white-walled chapel in which there are little brightly painted statues of Teresa and John of the Cross. The nuns sang to me—a custom that has come down from the time of Teresa, who as well as playing a drum and pipes used to make up verses and carols. When a humourless religious was scandalized to see *La Madre* taken up with such trivialities, Teresa rebuked her gently: 'We need all this to make life livable.' *Todo es menester para pasar esta vida.*[1]

The convent was gay. The Franciscan monastery, on the other hand, which is hidden among oaks and chestnut trees, I found melancholy—the more so, perhaps, because I saw it in the company of a blind friar who tapped his way pathetically over the marble floor of an ornate rococo chapel that could scarcely be less appropriate to the wild beauty of the *sierra* or the austerity of Peter of Alcántara in whose honour it was built. In the sacristy, as well as embroidered vestments and cruci-

[1] See Appendix, p. 182.

fixes of ivory and nacre, there is a block of wood that this most eccentric of saints fixed into the wall of his cell to serve as a pillow. For forty years, Teresa says, he did not sleep for more than one and a half hours a night; even then he was sitting upright, for his cell was too small for him to lie down. He was accustomed, moreover, to eat only once in three days. When Teresa expressed astonishment at this, he assured her that he had formed the habit without difficulty. He looked, which is not to be wondered at, 'as if he were made out of the roots of trees'. In cold weather he used to leave the door and the window of his cell open, then take off his sackcloth cloak so that presently he would have the satisfaction of putting it on again. However hot the sun or heavy the rain, he never covered his head. One time he lived for three years in a monastery of his Order without raising his eyes from the ground. He did not know a single one of his brethren by sight and could find his way about the house only by following in the steps of the others. When he saw that his life was drawing to its close, he repeated the psalm: *Laetatus sum in his quae dicta sunt mihi*; then knelt down and died. He was, Teresa says, very affable.

     *   *   *

The authority of the Bishop of Ávila, along with the Brief from Rome, was sufficient for the foundation of the convent. Nevertheless it was indiscreet to act without the sanction of the Provincial of the Carmelite Order. Teresa knew this, but fearing he would stand in her way, she decided to press on in secret. Fortunately, or in her words because the Lord arranged it, her brother-in-law, Juan de Ovalle, who was staying in Ávila, fell ill. As his wife was at home in Alba de Tormes, Teresa had permission to be absent from the Incarnation to nurse him. The time left over from attending to her patient she spent making ready the convent—instructing workmen and putting in such furniture as was needed.

On August 24th, the feast of Saint Bartholomew, the Blessed

Sacrament was placed in the convent and four nuns given the habit in the presence of Teresa, her sister Juana, her brother-in-law and a few friends. 'So,' she writes, 'with full weight of authority this convent of the most glorious Saint Joseph was founded in the year 1562.'

Then came the reaction. What, she asked herself, was the Provincial going to say? Would the nuns at Saint Joseph's be content? Had she not been foolish, as many persons had told her, to have had anything to do with the matter? Would her health stand the new life? Did she want to leave the Incarnation —give up her friends to live with persons whom she might not find to her liking? Had she not taken on a task beyond her strength? Was not the whole thing the work of the devil, to disturb her tranquillity, to make prayer impossible?

For a while she was in great distress. Then, after she had prayed before the Blessed Sacrament, the devil fled. She was able to laugh, realizing the mood was of his making.

Her troubles, however, were not ended. She was going to rest after dinner (she had scarcely slept the previous night) when she received a summons to go immediately to the Superior of the Incarnation. In a sense she cared little. She had done what she set out to do. She almost hoped they would put her into the convent prison; at least she would not have to talk to anyone—she was worn out with talking. She was told, however, that she must give an account of herself before the Provincial who was coming there and then. Though feeling that she had committed no offence either against God or the Carmelite Order, since her only desire was that the Rule should be observed with greater perfection, she nevertheless acknowledged her fault, thinking how Christ at his trial did not defend himself, and that to others, who did not know all the facts, her actions might well seem blameworthy. It was unjust that they should say she had tried to win esteem for herself. On the other hand, it certainly seemed absurd that she, who had herself failed to keep the rules of the Incarnation, should propose to live by a stricter rule. So, assuming an air of distress, that she might not appear to make light of the accusations, she begged the Provincial to punish her if he must, but not to go on being annoyed. After rebuking her in the presence of the community he told her privately that, once the commotion had died down, she had his sanction to join the other nuns at Saint Joseph's.

There was, indeed, a commotion. The Mayor of Ávila, the Councillors and the cathedral Chapter held a meeting in which it was decided that, since the existence of the convent was detrimental to the city's welfare, the Blessed Sacrament should be removed. They also called a meeting of the religious Orders to which two representatives came from each. These were either loud in condemnation or else silent—with the exception of Padre Ibáñez who without taking sides pointed out that the matter should be gone into with the greatest care—that in any case it was the affair of the Bishop.

People could talk of nothing else. They were busy, too, going backwards and forwards with their grievances to the Incarnation and the Provincial. Matters even reached the point of legal proceedings. The city sent delegates to Madrid with a report to go before the Royal Council, while Gonzalo de Aranda, a priest of Ávila and a friend of Teresa (she calls him 'a great servant of God and a lover of all perfection'), went on behalf of the convent. The dispute was prolonged by the fact that Teresa, basing her decision on the Primitive Rule of Carmel and on what she believed to be a command of Christ, was determined that the foundation should be without an endowment. In this she was supported by Peter of Alcántara, but opposed by Padre Ibáñez who in a letter two pages long, full of refutations and theological arguments, tried to prove to her that she was in error.

Finally, the matter was settled out of court. 'When we began to say the Office,' she writes, 'the people began to be very much attached to the convent. More nuns were received, and the Lord began to move the persons who had persecuted us

most, to help us and give us alms. So now they found themselves approving what before they had violently condemned
and by degrees they abandoned the lawsuit and said they
realized the work was of God.'

Teresa's Reform has survived the centuries. Convents of
Discalced Carmelites living by her Rule have been founded
even within the last decade in Europe, America and Japan.
The convent at Arenas de San Pedro is one of these modern
Carmels. Indeed, I found it easier at Arenas to imagine Saint
Joseph's as it must have been in Teresa's day than I did at Saint
Joseph's itself. The Foundress of Saint Joseph's had drawn her
inspiration from the ancient Rule of Carmel, but her mind was
on the immediate present and the future. Teresa was not a
person to live in the past. Had she belonged to this century she
would certainly have taken advantage of what science has to
offer. She would have been consulting a psychologist about the
melancholic Beatriz de la Madre de Dios. Instead of travelling
up and down Spain in a mule-cart, she would have been flying
across the world in an aeroplane.

Saint Joseph's in 1568 was young: it had no past. Now, it is
very old; older, I thought, than the Incarnation. It seems to be
encrusted with its past. The nuns, with their clinking rosaries
and sandals slapping on the flagstones, seemed to have come
up out of the centuries—to have wakened from sleep to do me
the courtesy of telling me about their Foundress. When I had
gone, they would slip back again—like the lizards I had watched
in the garden darting for a moment into sunlight, then back
into their holes. All their talk was of *la Santa Madre*—as if she
were someone among them still, who had gone out for a while
and might at any moment return. This was her chair. There
was the nut-tree she planted. Here was the inkpot that she used
when she wrote the *Way of Perfection*. The nun who told me
these things spoke a smattering of English. She punctuated her
remarks with a little laugh that seemed to be meant for herself,
as if she was telling herself how amusing it all was. Though I

visited the Incarnation many times, I did not go back to Saint Joseph's. Not even with the Bishop's authority, did I feel I could disturb these nuns from their past a second time.

*   *   *

There is a tradition that when Teresa left the Incarnation to live at Saint Joseph's, she first went barefoot down into the darkness of the crypt of the church of San Vicente, and before the candle-lit shrine of la Virgen de la Soterraña dedicated herself to the service of Christ and his Mother. From that day she ceased to be Doña Teresa de Cepeda y Ahumada. She had become Teresa de Jesús.

She wore a rough frieze habit, a white cloak and hempen sandals. She swept and cooked, sewed and worked at the distaff. It was her intention that her nuns should work. 'The religious should not ask for alms, unless under pressure of real necessity,' she laid down in the *Constitutions* of the Reform. 'Let them rather endeavour to support themselves by the labour of their hands.' Again she says: 'My daughters, strive to serve his Majesty so faithfully that you will not eat the bread of the poor unearned.' Apart from the necessity of work, if the community was to survive, she knew its psychological value. 'I wish our house had a bigger garden,' she writes at a later date, of the Seville convent, 'that sister Beatriz might have more to occupy her.' Even with the large garden at Saint Joseph's, food was often scarce. For that reason, the hour for dinner was not rigid; it depended on 'what the Lord might provide'. If there was something to eat, the bell was to be rung at half past eleven in winter; in summer, at ten o'clock.

Teresa had much business to attend to concerning the newly-founded convent, as well as accounts to do and letters to write. She talked to innumerable persons—workmen, noblemen, clerics, townspeople, relations. In addition, she finished the *Life* which she had begun at Toledo when staying with Doña Luisa de la Cerda. In a letter to the Dominican, García de

Toledo, to whom she is sending the manuscript (she says she is entrusting him with her 'soul') she explains that she has been too busy to read it over. She also wrote the *Way of Perfection*. She was working harder than she had ever worked, but because she was happy, she was in better health than ever before. She used to look back to these years at Saint Joseph's as the most peaceful in her life.

*   *   *

It was a time, too, during which she saw visions. I will mention only one.

The rain was beating down one morning with such violence that for a moment she doubted whether she would be able to get to the church for Mass. And yet, she knew that had the raindrops been spears levelled against her breast, still she would have gone. When she reached the church it was as if the heavens had opened. She saw the throne of God upheld by the Four Beasts, and a multitude of angels of such radiance that they seemed to be all afire. She felt within her a glory that could not be put into speech or writing, or conceived of in the mind. All things that can be desired were there, and yet there was nothing. They told her—she cannot say who told her—that all she could do was to understand that she was unable to understand anything. Then she heard the clock strike. She had been in the church for two hours. I used to wonder, in Ávila, where it was that Teresa saw this vision. Was it in the Jesuit church of San Gil, of which now only ruins remain? Or the splendid church of Santo Tomás? Or the dark austere San Pedro? I felt a conviction—for which I had no evidence—that it was in San Pedro. I never went into this church without thinking of the angels that 'seemed to be all afire'.

*   *   *

Writing for her nuns at Saint Joseph's, Teresa says in the *Way of Perfection*: 'Let us strive to live in such a way that our prayers may be of avail to help those servants of God, who at the cost of so much toil have fortified themselves with learning and virtuous living and have laboured to help the Lord.'

Francisco de Osuna taught that love is within the scope of every human being. So, then, is prayer. For prayer is an act of love. Teresa speaks of prayer as a loving conversation, yet one in which words are not an essential. As she well knew, in sickness or distress of mind, not only words but thought becomes impossible. Yet, even then, prayer is not excluded. The afflictions, whether of mind or body, become an offering of love. All that is needed is the will to love. Nor are those debarred from prayer whose thoughts are a turmoil of doubts and distractions, like horses that will not be disciplined. No matter how great the turmoil, persons so afflicted, if their will is set on God, will find in the depths of the soul, at a level untouched by the senses, a pool of peace. These, moreover, far from being worse off than others who are lifted to the heights of contemplation, are to be envied, sheltered as they are from the temptation to arrogance, from delusion and deception. They love without visible reward for their loving, proving their love in the darkness of humility. They are like the little donkeys that with eyes covered draw the water-wheel, not knowing the service that they are doing their master.

Teresa treats of prayer on many levels. She writes of vocal prayer, the prayer of quiet, the prayer of recollection, the prayer of union. To a reader like myself, unversed in mystical theology, these labels confuse rather than help. But she did not intend great importance to be attached to them. Prayer is not to be divided into rigid compartments. In the *Interior Castle* she says that it is not to be thought that there are only the seven Mansions which she describes—in fact there are thousands, 'some above, some below, others at each side.' What, however, does stand out in her writing on prayer is the fact that at no level, not even when she treats of the highest union that is possible between the soul and God, is there any severance between earth and heaven. The soul that has soared to God is still tethered to earth as if by a thread of such delicacy that it is not felt as a hindrance, of such strength that it cannot be broken. Prayer never becomes a vague intoxication as it did in the case of her contemporaries, the *Alumbrados* or Illuminists, who regarded it as being so divorced from the material world that to meditate on Christ's manhood was a barrier to perfect contemplation. For Teresa, the Word made Flesh is the pivot and the object of prayer. This is one of the reasons why Protestants, who sometimes are scandalized by what they feel to be, in the Catholic Church a too great emphasis on Christ's Mother and the saints, are drawn to Teresa. They see demonstrated in her that fellowship between the soul and Christ which is the ideal of Protestantism.

If, however, prayer is centred in Christ, it is also made subject to the Church that he founded on earth to be the guardian of truth. Teresa, when she came to die, gave thanks that she was a daughter of the Church. In her view no vision, locution or mystical experience of any kind can be of God if it runs counter to the Church's teaching. Better, she says, to forgo all spiritual consolations than to deny one iota of this teaching. She stresses, too, that those who believe themselves drawn to God by the perilous way of contemplative prayer stand in need of direction. That they may not delude themselves or be deluded by the devil, they need the help of learned men to guide them— if these are spiritual persons so much the better, but learned they must be, since 'learning throws a light on many things'. The idea of spiritual direction goes back to the beginning of Christianity. The disciples said to their master: 'Lord, teach us to pray.' But it goes further back still. Socrates, in the *Crito*, teaches that in matters concerning the soul no less than in those of the body the guidance of an expert is necessary. Teresa set such store by this that she used to obey her confessor before the commands of Christ that came to her in a vision. In the latter case she realized the possibility of self-deception. On the other hand she had no illusions as to the havoc that can be wrought by stupid or ignorant directors.

Again, the soul may be thought of as tethered to the earth in the sense that prayer is inseparable from the practice of the virtues. It is more

> 'Than an order of words, the conscious occupation
> Of the praying mind, or the sound of the voice praying.'

So, when the soul has ascended to the seventh Mansion, where, face to face with God, it is granted a foretaste of the Beatific Vision, it must of necessity drop back again to earth to busy itself in the service of God's servants. Works, works, works, is Teresa's reiterated cry. Did Saint Paul shut himself up with his visions, enjoying divine favours, pursuing no occupation? No, he rested not a single day, nor at night either—at night he was earning his living. And the woman of Samaria to whom Christ spoke at the well? Did she spend the rest of her life dreaming her days away? No, she went back to her village and told what she had heard to others, that they too might learn. And, woman though she was—and not an important one either— she was believed. Teresa admired the woman of Samaria. She thought her clever to have found an audience. Also, she was humble; she was not annoyed, as many persons would have been, when Christ pointed out her faults.

The ancients believed that only by humility could man escape the visitation of blind, inexorable fate. For the Christian, to be humble is to trust God infinitely. Of the three virtues which Teresa declares are inseparable from prayer—love, detachment and humility—she puts humility as the first, because, she says, it comprises the others. She calls it the 'salve of all our wounds': *el ungüento de nuestras heridas*. Without it, the other virtues can be a cause for vanity. Remembering the games of chess that she played as a girl with her brothers, she says that humility is the queen of the virtues by whom alone the King of Heaven will allow himself to be made a prisoner.

Humility drew God down from heaven into the Virgin's womb. By humility we, too, can draw him into our souls.

Humility pertains primarily to man in his relation to God; detachment, in his relation to creatures. To be detached is not to turn away from creation, but to see it for what it is. It is to enjoy an inner freedom, to know that nothing, not persons, nor wealth nor honour nor power, not the wonders of nature nor the arts, not any created thing can satisfy a soul created to find satisfaction only in God. Writing as she is for the nuns of Saint Joseph's, she inculcates detachment through simple examples. Relations are not to be encouraged to visit the convent. 'Detach yourself from your relations,' she says, 'and you will find parents and brothers and sisters where you never thought to find them.' This injunction must be seen in the context of Spain (particularly the Spain of her century) where family ties and obligations go beyond anything that we are now accustomed to in this country. It is not easy, even if a person should wish it, to be free of relatives, if only because these are so numerous. I remember the parlour of a Franciscan convent in Madrid on a Sunday afternoon—the crowd of people talking, or waiting to talk, at the grille. Relations, I was told. In Teresa's day at the Incarnation, there was no end to the visits from relations—many of them coming for no better reason than to bring or pick up a piece of tasty gossip.

What she says must not, however, be taken in isolation. Hardly has she stressed the point that relatives are not to be encouraged than she is making exceptions. Parents—and the same applies to brothers and sisters—must not be turned away if they feel the need to come; they must be helped and comforted. We know from her letters, as well as scattered remarks through her other writings, that hours of time were given to helping her relations, even to the extent of looking after the affairs of her brother. She writes to Lorenzo; 'My experiences with these houses of God and the Order have made me so good at bargains and business deals that I am well up in everything, so

I can handle your affairs as if they were those of the Order, and am delighted to be able to attend to them.'

There is no complacency in Teresa's conception of the religious life; no suggestion that those who live it are better than their brothers and sisters in the world. What matters, she says, is not whether or no we wear the habit, but whether we practise the virtues and surrender our will to God's. She warns her nuns against comparing one person with another—a hateful practice: *cosa odiosa*. They are to remember that those who are punctilious themselves are apt to be shocked at others who live differently, yet, from the latter important lessons can be learnt; 'There is no reason why we should expect everyone to travel by our road, nor should we attempt to point out the spiritual path, when perhaps we do not know what it is.'

More important than detachment from relatives is detachment from self. It is no virtue to hide illness that is real, but to be always thinking about trivial ailments is a mistake. Such things come and go, and are best ignored. Complaining about them only becomes a habit—so much so that one day a nun is absenting herself from choir because she has had a headache a while ago, another day because she has just had one, and on the next for fear she may have it again; yet a married woman will put up with serious troubles sooner than upset her husband. Again, she urges her nuns to give no thought to the niceties of honour and precedence. May God preserve us from such preoccupations! She knew only too well the weaknesses of her countrymen in such matters, coming as she did from a family that prided itself on its aristocratic lineage: *la limpia sangre*. She confesses to have been worn out sometimes trying to remember the points of etiquette to be observed in addressing the great ones of the world—who should be called Magnificent, who Illustrious. In the universities it was no better than elsewhere. A man who had studied theology must not demean himself by taking a course in philosophy. He must go up, never down. In convents it was the same. A nun who has been a Prioress is affronted if asked to hold a humbler office. May God deliver us from persons who, thinking they live the religious life, are punctilious in matters of honour and sensitive to insult! Better they should keep their honour and stay at home, for in a convent such an attitude spreads like foam on water. Better the convent go up in flames than there be in it nuns who say: 'I'm in the right,' or 'I am longer in the Order,' or 'I am older,' or—still worse—repeat by way of charity some insult whether real or imaginary, adding: 'Fancy letting yourself be treated like this,' or 'You are just a beast of burden,' or 'may God give you patience! A saint could not endure more.'

Writing of spiritual love Teresa says that those who love in this way do not love less than others, but more. They may find pleasure in a person's appearance, but they are not content with this; to be so would seem to them to be loving the unsubstantial, a shadow that will pass. Their eyes look through the body into the soul. If they see there even a glint of gold they will dig deep in search of more, sparing themselves no pain.

Love, on its highest level, can be purely spiritual, but this is rare. More often there is in it an element of the sensual. Teresa confesses that she finds it almost impossible to tell whether love is wholly spiritual or not. In any case, this is not important. The sensual should not be despised; it, too, can be turned into a virtue. In making this point she touches on the relationship between a nun and her confessor. If she imagines she has too great an affection for him, there is no need to be attacked by a battery of scruples and to go searching for someone else, only to find the same thing happening again. Provided the confessor is leading her to greater perfection, she should not bother about being fond of him. It would be worse, since he is doing her much service, if she were to feel nothing for him in return. In her own experience, she has found it a help to be attached to her confessor. 'So weak are we that such affection helps us considerably to undertake great things in God's service.' If, however, he should show any wrongful intention—and anyone with a grain of sense can see if this is so—she should ask to go to someone else, but being careful in this to observe discretion so as not to injure his reputation.

Teresa always writes out of her own experience. From her childhood to the end of her life she loved intensely and on many levels. She loved, in particular, her mother and her brothers, her sister Juana and, most of all, her father. In adolescence she experienced love of a different kind, outside the immediate circle of her family—love which, with the older relative, came near to an infatuation—but, as well as this, the first awakening of romantic love for someone of the other sex. At the time of her illness there was her affection for the priest of Becedas. Then, following her illness, the attachments of the *locutorio*. When, after much conflict of mind, these ended with a suddenness that was nothing short of dramatic, it would not have been surprising if Teresa, with her Spanish propensity for extremes— *todo o nada*—had cut herself off entirely from human contacts. Indeed, a few isolated remarks towards the end of the *Life* might lead one to suppose that this was so. But her writings must be read in conjunction one with another. As well as the *Foundations*, in which she writes frequently of friends and acquaintances, her letters make it plain that the circle of persons for whom she had a deep affection continued to widen as her life went on. She extended that Christian charity, which makes it possible to love in Christ even those whom we cannot like, to a host of people of every calling, from royalty to muleteers, including Don Pedro, her neurotic brother, the unpredictable and dangerous Princess of Éboli, and the hysterical Beatriz de la Madre de Dios. Over and above these, like tall flowers standing up from a meadow, were those whom she loved with a special love; among them, her brother Lorenzo; Doña Luisa de la Cerda, María de San José, Prioress of Seville, and more than all Padre Gracián.

It is unlikely that anyone who has laid down principles of behaviour for others has consistently lived up to these. Certainly, Teresa was the last person to regard herself as a model to be imitated. More so perhaps even than most human beings, Teresa is a mass of apparent inconsistencies. Her writing seems to contradict itself. She says, for example, in the *Way of Perfection* that spiritual love at its highest should be untouched by passion. A little further on she writes: 'Do you think that such persons [those who love spiritually] will love none and delight in none except God? No, they love others much more than they did, with a genuine love, with greater passion: *con más pasión*.' Here, as so often, the inconsistency is only apparent. Teresa is using the word passion in different senses. In the second instance the word has a sense as far removed from its usual meaning as Pentecostal fire from the fires of nature.

Again, in the *Way of Perfection*, she would appear in one passage to imply that the wish to be loved is an imperfection. Yet the letters make it abundantly clear that not only did Teresa want affection from those she loved, but that she never attempted to pretend otherwise. She asks Gracián if he does not love her as much as his mother? After all, she, Teresa, needs his love more—his mother has other members of her family, but she herself has only her 'dear father in God'.

Had this discrepancy between her teaching and her life been pointed out to her, she would certainly have replied that the fact that she did not herself practise what she preached was no reason not to preach; that her nuns, being more perfect than she was, might well rise to heights to which she could never attain. In any case, it has to be borne in mind that Teresa in the *Way of Perfection* was doing no more than laying down general principles for the guidance of her nuns, many of them young girls by no means without intelligence but with little education; daughters, too, of Castile, with a military tradition at their back, wanting from their Foundress orders to obey in the service of the King of Heaven as clear-cut as those given to their fathers and brothers in the armies of Philip.

Teresa's orders—if I may use such a word, for they are

exhortations rather than commands—are clear but not rigid.
Meals, for instance, are not normally to be served in convent
parlours: if everyone were to be fed, the nuns would starve.
For Gracián, however, an exception is to be made; it is only
reasonable in the case of a Superior—besides, he needs looking
after. Incidentally, when his mother paid a visit to Toledo,
Teresa had meals sent out to her from the convent to the house
where she was staying.

Similarly in regard to love. As a general principle Teresa
tells her daughters not to ask to be loved in return. There is,
however, another point to be remembered. Teresa, as she
grew older, became more gentle; more tolerant both of others
and of herself. In her youth there had been traces of something
that comes nearer to Stoicism than Christianity—a straining
and forcing of the personality that certainly contributed to her
illness. As the years went by she became increasingly more ready
to accept herself as she was—in all that was not sin, knowing
that God who understands all else will understand this also.
Gradually, she had come to see that, since God asks for the love
of his creatures, it is not for his children to turn their backs on
love. Shall the servant be greater than the master?

4

Medina del Campo · Valladolid
El Escorial

I WAS sorry to be leaving Ávila. I would miss the red-billed storks flapping their wings against the sky; the roar of voices in the *plaza*; the quiet, cobbled streets—so quiet at night that walking through them I could hear the clink of the watchman's keys. I was content in the hotel Reina Isabel, where my room with its uncarpeted floor and a crucifix over the bed was hardly less austere than a convent cell. Austere but not quiet. Doors slammed in the night, footsteps clattered in corridors; from the railway station engines gave a shrill, demented cry.

I had become used to the friendly but not imposing Carmelite church, with the statue of Teresa, richly robed, bedecked with jewels and crowned with brass, set in an ornate rococo shrine that bore on it the words *Aquí nació Santa Teresa de Jesús*. It is a much revered statue but, in my view, inferior to the little figure roughly carved in wood that is preserved in the Biblioteca Teresiana, in the palace of the Marqués de Benevita— possibly the first image to be made of the saint.

I would miss the Incarnation; and the hermitage of San Segundo candle-lit and shadowy, hung with votive offerings of wax masks in honour of Santa Lucia who, for a reason I do not know, has ousted the saint and bishop to whom this little church is dedicated. I would miss the garden of San Roque; the lovers and the children; the mountains winged with snow; and, when the sun dropped, the purple glow of twilight sweeping up from the plain, lapping city walls that are become, all at

99

once, as pale as rice-paper and scarcely more substantial; and, overhead, the first star glimmering.

* * *

I looked back at the walls, from the train. In the hard sunlight they were a rich, baked brown. I thought them friendly, in contrast to the desolation of a landscape strewn with boulders that might have been flung there in some primeval cataclysm. Growing among the boulders were tall, rough grasses and spiky broom or a ragged fir tree or dark, shiny hollies. As time went on the rocks became fewer, until there was only the plain—ochre and emerald and shadowed with purple, stretching away to where the *sierra* held up an immense sky that was a pale, washed blue, flecked with little clouds like wisps of wool.

It had seemed as if Teresa would end her days at Saint Joseph's. This, however, was not to be. In April 1567 Fray Juan Bautista Rubeo, General of the Carmelite Order, came to see her at the convent. He had come to Ávila after making a visitation in Andalusia, where he was so angered by the slackness among the religious that he exiled some of them from the province, imprisoned others and sent others to the galleys. He ransacked the friars' cells, removing anything he found that was forbidden by the Constitutions. Teresa was apprehensive, not because he was likely to disapprove of Saint Joseph's, but because, owing to irregularities in its foundation, it had been put under the jurisdiction not of the Carmelite Order, but of the Bishop. She need not have been alarmed. After she had told her story simply and truthfully (this, she says, was her way in dealing with prelates) and had shown him the Constitutions she had drawn up, Rubeo gave her authority to found in Castile— but not in Andalusia—as many convents as there were hairs on her head. Later, he sent her from Barcelona a licence to found two houses for friars.

The distances in Spain are tremendous; the landscape not

only desolate, but often savage. I preferred travelling by train
rather than by car. A train provides that sense of security which
people found long ago, and still find in some parts of the world,
by moving in large numbers. As well as the passengers—and
Spaniards are particularly ready to draw a stranger into their
conversation and to share whatever they have, whether sweets,
fruit or even an entire meal—there are the Civil Guard;
usually two of them going up and down the corridor, wearing
tricorne hats and white gloves, rifles slung over their shoulders.
I remember the pair on the train north from Ávila. They came
into the carriage for a while and sat rolling cigarettes—one of
them lean with a melancholy Don Quixote face, the other
plump. It worried them to find that I was not the wife of a
Frenchman sitting opposite me; still more, that I was travelling
alone. 'Sola?' they said one after the other, sadly.

Teresa, when she went out to make her foundations, generally travelled in a covered mule-cart with heavy wooden
wheels and no springs. Occasionally she rode and was known
for her good seat. Gracián says of her that she was as at home on
the back of a mule as in a carriage. At Saint Joseph's I was shown
a saddle that she used on at least one journey between Medina
del Campo and Ávila, a distance of approximately eighty
miles. In a letter written to her friend Doña Luisa de la Cerda,
she mentions having borrowed a saddle belonging to her ladyship. As well as the nuns who went with her for the foundation
she was intending to make, she had an escort mounted on
horses and mules—a necessary precaution against brigands—
made up of laymen and two or three clergy: among them, as a
rule, was the faithful Julián de Ávila, the first chaplain of Saint
Joseph's, whose account of the journeys supplements her own.
On one occasion when going from Seville to Malagón in the
heat of midsummer, her brother Lorenzo provided an open
carriage. Teresa was delighted. She writes to Gracián: 'It was a
much better idea than coming in covered carts.' This harmless
innovation gave rise, however, to talk. People in Toledo said

that she was a frivolous woman who travelled round the country with fine ladies and gallants.

Her journeys were formidable: in summer, burning sun and drought; in winter, ice and snow and floods. The roads, which at their best were hardly more than a track cutting across the plain or following the slopes of the mountains, were often impassable. The inns were appalling; infested with vermin and crowded with adventurers, soldiers and mule-drivers. Julián de Ávila mentions how in one the floor was covered with sleeping muleteers so that it was impossible for the nuns to move without treading on either bodies or harness. The only thing to be said in favour of such places was the fact that, when it was time to leave, everyone was in high spirits.

When the heat was intense it was sometimes found preferable to travel through the night. On one such journey between Ávila and Salamanca, in July 1573, Teresa became separated from the rest of the party. She eventually appeared in the company of a labourer whom she had paid four *reales* to put her on her way. During this same journey a donkey was lost that was carrying on its back the sum of one thousand five hundred ducats—the dowry of Ana de Jesús intended for the purchase of a house. In the morning the animal was found lying a little distance off the road, the money intact.

The plain of Castile reaches on and on, hour after hour. From time to time its monotony is broken by a plantation of evergreen oaks with black, writhing branches. A village is as rare as an oasis in a desert and, when it comes, is hardly more than a handful of mud-coloured hovels, clustering as if for protection round a church that looks absurdly large.

There is little sign of life. An eagle hovers, tawny-winged, lost in the sky's immensity. A crow with plumage that glints a vivid, metallic blue, rises; then drops again. A shepherd watches over sheep the colour of stones. A rider wearing a wide-brimmed hat reins in his horse, then shades his eyes to watch the train. I remember the delay at little, sleepy Peñaranda while the station master, wearing a gold and scarlet cap worthy of a general in the Peninsular war, wrangled with a peasant woman about a goat. As we waited I could see the sandy road that strikes across the plain to Duruelo, where Teresa established her first house for friars—that 'little Bethlehem', as she calls it in the *Foundations*. When she broke her journey there on the way to Toledo in February 1569 she found Fray Antonio de Heredia, formerly Prior of the monastery of Santa Ana, at Medina del Campo, sweeping the porch, his face wreathed in smiles: *con un rostro de alegría*. 'What has become of your dignity, father?' she said to him. 'I rue the day I had any,' was his reply. With her were two friends of hers, merchants from Medina. When they saw the crosses and skulls in the little church they could do nothing but weep.

The villages and towns of the plain have gracious, musical names; Peñaranda and Duruelo; Fontiveros and Madrigal de las Altas Torres; Ávila and Arévalo. I remember mediaeval, rock-built Arévalo, where John of the Cross was apprenticed to a woodcarver and a painter, its towers and castle burnished by the evening sun. I remember, too, the castle at Medina del Campo standing up, alone, on the far horizon; seeming, as it drew nearer, to bring the past with it; and then, as it receded till it was no more than a speck on the skyline, to take the past away again.

Medina del Campo has a great, black echoing station. There is what calls itself a *fonda* and outside it on the platform a few tables and chairs. I never saw anyone at these tables—nor, indeed, anyone on the platform, except one grilling day in August when a couple of railway men, stripped to the waist, were sluicing themselves under a pump. If a Spaniard were to write a *Ghost Train*, the setting ought to be the station at Medina.

The town is a sleepy place of cobbled streets, geranium-coloured brick walls, churches and monasteries. It has a shabby dignity, yet little that recalls its history or a prosperity so great that the profits made by a single merchant, on one day of its world-famed *feria*, were enough to build a hospital. It is rich, too, in associations with John of the Cross. He learnt to read and write in a school for small children run by nuns—he was remembered afterwards as a 'fine, quick little fellow'; *muy bonito y muy agudo*. From the age of fourteen or possibly fifteen, until he was twenty-one, he worked in the hospital either of the Concepción or San Antonio, at the same time attending classes in grammar at the Jesuit college. He received the habit of a Carmelite in the church of Santa Ana.

The convent Teresa founded is in the sixteenth-century Calle de Santiago. Iron-studded doors open under a key-stone arch into a porch, on whose walls are charcoal drawings of herself and Saint Albert, the Carmelite. In the sacristy, with its high barred windows, I held in my hands Teresa's breviary, a fat book printed in Gothic lettering. I was also shown an account book with each item entered in her bold handwriting, and at the foot of the page the total expenditure followed by her signature. Among the entries for the year 1571 is the price of a pair of shoes bought for the mother of John of the Cross, Catalina Álvarez, who is buried under a vault in the cloisters.

* * *

Teresa was fifty-one when she left Ávila for Medina del Campo on August 15th, 1568. She had authority on her side, but that did not mean that her enterprise was looked upon with favour. There was, she says, a great deal of uncharitable talk. Some people said that she was out of her mind. Even the Bishop, who since the founding of Saint Joseph's had been most kindly disposed, thought her action the height of folly, but refrained from saying so for fear of causing her distress. She had to borrow money for the journey, and more to pay the rent of the house that Julián de Ávila had found in advance at the rent of 51,000 *maravedís* a year. Now, as in the future, she troubled little about money, confident that what was needed would somehow be forthcoming. Nor did she allow herself to be dismayed by the difficulties that lay ahead—she had faced too many in the founding of Saint Joseph's. Nevertheless she met with plenty of discouragement. When they reached Arévalo, after travelling all through the day, there was a letter from the landlord of the house at Medina telling them not to come; he had decided not to let the house after all, for fear of annoying his neighbours, the Augustinians, who were prepared to go to law rather than allow the nuns to be installed. In spite of this, Teresa, after a night of much worry, decided to press on, leaving behind some of the nuns in a nearby village until she could see how matters would work out. However, as she was passing through Olmedo she learnt that a widow at Medina was willing to let her have a house, though in bad repair.

Julián de Ávila had gone ahead to warn the Carmelite fathers of Teresa's arrival. At midnight, he was thundering at the door of the monastery of Santa Ana. In the archives of the Order there still remains the record of money spent on a lamp and oil 'for the new convent', also on supper for the young men who had come with the nuns. Teresa and her companions got out of the mule-carts on the outskirts of the town, going the remainder of the way on foot to avoid drawing attention. She was in terror that the news of their arrival would leak out—in particular, that it might reach the ears of the Augustinians before she was installed in the house. In making her foundations it was her practice to take possession of a house at all costs, then face the difficulties. They made their way through deserted streets, feeling the more uneasy because it was the hour at which the bulls were being enclosed for the fight on the following day. However, they met only a few persons, who were content merely to make rude remarks—as well they might, for the party, laden with vestments and other things necessary for the Mass, looked like a pack of gypsies who had been robbing a church. They were fortunate in not being seen by a watchman, who would certainly have locked them up.

They reached their destination to find the house even more dilapidated than they had supposed. There were holes in the roof, and the walls were without plaster. Teresa and the nuns worked through what remained of the night, sweeping, scrubbing and hanging up bits of tapestry as well as a blue damask bedspread given them by the steward of the lady who owned the property. They had forgotten to bring nails, so had to make do with those they could find in the walls. It was so dark that sometimes they did not know if they were inside the building or out in the street. By daybreak they had set up an altar and hung a bell. Mass was said and the Blessed Sacrament reserved. The Lord thought fit, Teresa comments, that the Carmelite father should be blind—else he could never have allowed the Sacrament to remain in such surroundings.

In the daylight, the house was worse still. Part of the wall overlooking the courtyard was in ruins. Exhausted by travelling, anxiety and a sleepless night, Teresa began to lose heart. Had she done right in coming? Had she been deluded in supposing it to be God's will? There were the nuns to think of, who had come with her: they would be humiliated if they had to return to Ávila. To make matters worse, there was a certain amount of ill-feeling in Medina. Some people likened her to Magdalena de la Cruz, the crazy nun of Córdoba. Above all she was afraid that the Lutherans might steal the Blessed Sacrament. She had men to keep watch, but even so she was uneasy. She used to get up in the night and look through a window that faced on to the porch. She could see the Sacrament in the light of the moon.

The pattern of Saint Joseph's was repeating itself. There were the misgivings, the opposition. Then, as before, she took heart again. Gradually the opposition died down. People came, as they had in Ávila, with alms and offers of help. The Prior of the Carmelites undertook to have the house repaired. Meanwhile a merchant called Blas de Medina put the upper floor of his home at the disposal of the nuns until their own was ready. He also gave them his great gilded hall to be used as a chapel.

She was visited in this house by Antonio de Jesús and John of the Cross, then Juan de Matías—the men who were to be her first friars. The former, who played an important and a faithful role in the history of the Discalced, was nevertheless in some ways a tiresome man—self-important and inclined to take umbrage. Teresa had doubts as to his suitability—indeed, she looked upon his suggestion to join the Reform as a joke; he was nearly sixty and fastidious. John of the Cross, on the other hand, she took to her heart at once. She used to call him 'el Santico'—he was not more than five feet high—and because of his learning: 'mi Senequita'; my little Seneca. He is said to have put on the Discalced habit for the first time (it was made by the nuns out of coarse wool used for horse-cloths) in the parlour of the Medina convent in Teresa's presence. His brethren used to tease him, saying that he had been clothed by a woman.

Though the pattern of Saint Joseph's repeated itself, there was a difference. At Ávila, once the turmoil had died down, Teresa had been able to live in the convent she founded, enjoying an atmosphere of quiet and recollection. Never again, except for a while at Toledo, was she to have such peace. After only three months in Medina del Campo she was travelling again; first to Madrid, where she spent a fortnight with Doña Leonor de Mascareñas, formerly governess to Philip II and foundress of a Franciscan convent; then, to Alcalá de Henares for consultations with the Dominican theologian, Fray Domingo Báñez, and from there to Toledo to stay with Doña Luisa de la Cerda, while planning a foundation on the latter's estate at Malagón. No sooner was the Malagón convent established than Teresa came back to Ávila, breaking her journey at Escalona where she went under obedience to visit the Marquésa de Villena. She reached Ávila at the beginning of June 1568. On the last day of that month she was on her way

north to Valladolid. That was how her life was to be spent,
travelling when and where the Lord willed; constantly re-
tracing her steps; north, south, then north again, regardless of
distance or inclination.

*   *   *

It rained the whole way from Medina del Campo to Valladolid, cold driving rain that lashed the windows of the railway
carriage. The landscape was hardly more than a tawny blur
that cleared now and then to reveal a church belfry or poplar
trees or hills that were flat, as if the top of each had been sliced
off, and strangely pale.

When I came out of the station, the rain had stopped. The
sun breaking through the clouds fell on the silver-pale stone
of the cathedral. Outside a pavement café a waiter glanced
hopefully at the sky as he put up a crimson and white awning.

It was the week after Easter. Only a few nights before
I had stood in the dark streets of Ávila watching the Good
Friday procession. I had watched the children carrying before
them the symbols of the Passion—a miniature cross and ladder,
a hammer and nails, a spear, a scroll, a tunic, a reed and a
sponge. I had seen the penitents go by wearing their white
cone-shaped hats, their faces masked mysteriously. Behind
them the dead Christ was borne with great tenderness shoulder-
high among the crowd. Swaying lanterns flung their light upon
the pale body resting in a glass-sided coffin. A drum beat and
voices rose in solemn chanting. I waited by the Puerta del
Alcázar, the ramparts looming above me, as the procession
passed under the arched gateway, then wove its way through
the silent, crowded *plaza*. The hats of the penitents looked like
candle-snuffers. The flare of torches dimmed the stars.

In Ávila the Holy Week ceremonies are touching in their
simplicity. They remain today as they have been down the
centuries. Teresa could have seen what I saw. The ceremonies
in Valladolid, on the other hand, are renowned for their splen-

dour. People come to see them from all over Spain and beyond. The *pasos* takes hours to go by. I had missed all this. I saw only the palms hanging from windows and balconies, and in the churches the carved wooden figures, some of them still standing on the wheeled platforms on which they are drawn through the streets.

There was a Madonna with rings on her fingers, wearing a dress of stiff black brocade, and on her head a pointed halo of shining brass. Seven swords pierced her heart, and the tears on her cheeks glistened like raindrops. She stood above a cluster of gutted candles that might have been the stalks of flowers from which the petals had fallen. There was Christ praying in the garden, and nearby the disciples asleep; Christ at the pillar, the blood congealed upon his back; Christ with a reed in his hand and a rope about his neck; Christ on the cross and a thief on either side; Christ in the tomb, as one asleep, his head on a pillow, his flesh wax-pale, like a lotus flower.

'You should have been here for Holy Week,' people said to me.

'You should have seen the *pasos*.'

'¡Qué espectáculo!'

'¡Qué precioso!'

I had missed the pageantry, missed everything, it seemed. Yet the images standing there forgotten in the empty churches had a meaning of their own. They had had their glory. Their moment was past. Theirs was the loneliness of Christ when the hosannas of Palm Sunday were ended. I felt drawn into their loneliness. I was able to understand better why Teresa was moved by the *Ecce Homo* in the oratory at the Incarnation.

There were more images in the Museo de San Gregorio. More Christs and Virgins. And, besides these, a host of saints. There was John the Baptist, a fierce lonely figure. There was his head on a platter carved and painted with horrifying realism. There was John the Evangelist, his face the face of a visionary; and Peter, wild-haired and wild-eyed, with a countenance on which remorse and love were struggling for mastery. Teresa was there in the habit of a Carmelite, a quill in one hand and in the other a book. Simon Stock reached out his arms for the gift of the scapular. Saint Jerome looked incongruous in a cardinal's hat. Mary Magdalen, wearing a tunic plaited of palm-leaves, her long hair loose upon her shoulders, gazed in tender concern on the crucifix she held before her. Mary of Egypt was contemplating a skull.

That night I became ill with a fever. It was an attack of no great consequence, but alarming while it lasted. I tossed on my bed hour after hour in a state between waking and sleeping. The room seemed to be full of saints looking down at me with supercilious expressions. Saint Ignatius stood by my pillow, wearing black velvet embroidered with gold. Saint Isidro wore a leather jerkin and high boots; a yoke of oxen were at his side. John the Baptist kept changing his appearance with chameleon rapidity, becoming each time more formidable. Then I seemed to be out of doors, standing under a colonnade in the Plaza Mayor into which a mob was surging from the neighbouring streets. There were more people on balconies and at windows. On a platform raised above the crowd I saw Philip the King in a black doublet and hose. His face had a secretive expression and his hair was pale under his feathered cap. There was a savage roar of voices, then a silence more horrible than the shouting. Those condemned by the Inquisitors were filing past. They wore the yellow *sanbenito* painted with tongues of flame, and carried candles and green crosses. Presently, I was back in my room. Saint John of the Cross was there. He was wearing the white cloak of a Carmelite and his expression was at once ecstatic and compassionate. I heard over and over again the words:

Oh noche amable más que el alborada.
O night more lovely than the dawn.

I did not know whether it was he or myself who was saying

them. Then, I knew it was myself; and what I had thought to be his cloak was the curtain. Through the window I saw the sky streaked with daylight.

*　　*　　*

Teresa came to Valladolid in August 1568. The foundation had been hurried on in consequence of a revelation in which it was made known to her that the soul of Bernardino de Mendoza—he was the brother of the Bishop of Ávila—who had provided a house for the convent and died immediately afterwards—would be released from purgatory after the first Mass was said. The house, which was at Río de Olmos, a little way outside the city, had a fine garden and a vineyard. Its position by the river, however, was unhealthy, with the result that the nuns fell ill one by one with quartan fever. John of the Cross, who had nursed contagious diseases in the hospital at Medina, helped to look after them; he had come to Valladolid with Teresa to study the way of life under the Reform. A letter written to her friend Don Francisco de Salcedo shows how much she thought of him; it shows also, that there were sometimes differences of opinion: 'Small in stature though he is, I believe he is great in the sight of God. We shall certainly miss him sorely here, for he is a sensible person and well fitted for our way of life. . . . The Lord seems to be leading him by the hand, for, although we have had a few disagreements here over business matters and I have been the cause of them and have sometimes been vexed with him, we have never seen the least imperfection in him. He has courage.'

In due course, the community moved into the present convent, on the edge of the city. It has a great cobbled courtyard and an orchard enclosed by high walls. I saw here the manuscript of the *Way of Perfection*, written on quarto sheets in Teresa's bold sweeping hand, and preserved in a silver reliquary made in the shape of a book. This is her second revised version intended for a wider circle of readers than the first. The earlier one is in the library at the Escorial, in its original silk binding and decorated with little yellow flowers.

*　　*　　*

It is in connection with the Valladolid convent that Teresa tells the story of the eleven-year-old Casilda de Padilla, of one of the wealthiest families in Spain, who, while spending a happy day in the company of her betrothed, suddenly became downcast at the characteristically Spanish thought that the day would soon end, and so would all the days to come after. From that time, she was torn in two directions—loving her betrothed, yet 'inclining towards that which would never end'; believing too, that, if she became absorbed in worldly things, she would forget to strive for things eternal. Set on becoming a nun, she defied her relatives: one day when she was being taken for a drive in her grandmother's carriage, she eluded her governess and slipped into the Discalced convent. Neither her grandmother nor her mother, nor her uncle nor her prospective bridegroom could prevail on her to come out. Eventually, a Royal Order was obtained to have her removed. Even this was not the end of the story. A short time after she was taken home, she again eluded her governess while they were in church together. 'She stuck her overshoes up her sleeves, caught up her skirt and ran with the greatest possible haste' in the direction of the convent. Her governess rushed after her, shouting. Casilda was too quick. She darted in the outer door of the convent, then called to the nuns to let her into the enclosure. There was no coming out this time. 'May God be blessed,' Teresa ends, 'who can make one for so long a lover of rich dresses, happy in poor garments of frieze.'

*　　*　　*

The auto-de-fé in the presence of Philip, about which I had dreamt, took place in the autumn of 1559, nearly ten years before Teresa came to Valladolid. The Inquisition is there,

always, in the background of her life. In 1576, Bartolomé de
Carranza, Archbishop of Toledo, a man honoured for his
learning and his goodness, died exhausted in mind and body
after seventeen years of imprisonment. In the same year, Luis
de León, poet and philosopher and one of the most distin-
guished minds in the Church of that day, was thrown into
prison and left there for five years. Saint John of the Cross came
under suspicion. So did the mystic, Luis de Granada; and the
well-known preacher Juan de Ávila, the 'apostle of Andalusia'.
In the latter years of her life Teresa was in constant dread of
what might happen to Gracián, particularly when he was in
Andalusia where the Inquisition had its headquarters. She
mentions her fear of 'the Angels', as she used to call the Inquisitors: 'el miedo de los Ángeles.' She refers, too, to Gracián's own
alarm when one day, while he was at Paterna near Seville, a
party of Inquisitors drove up in a carriage to the convent door.

Before the founding of Saint Joseph's Teresa had laughed
when friends had warned her that she might be summoned
to give an account of herself. At that time she had written
nothing. It was another matter when the Life, much of which
is a record of her mystical experiences, was being widely
talked of. When she was told in 1575 that the book had been
denounced to the Inquisition—possibly through the Princess
of Éboli—she showed considerable distress. Padre Báñez, her
confessor, who was also disturbed on her behalf, decided that
the wisest course was to hand the manuscript to the Inquisition
himself—which he did, after making a few emendations. It
was kept for some time, then returned with permission for it
to be circulated among the convents of the Reform.

The Life probably escaped condemnation because of the
tone in which it is written. All that she says is clothed in expressions of such humility that the most exacting judge could
scarcely have taken exception. As well as declaring that her
spiritual favours are as nothing compared to obedience to the
Church, she speaks of herself as an ignorant, unlettered woman,

always ready to submit to the judgment of learned men. In short, she disarms the Inquisitors, as she did all who would lord it over others, with a gentle, ironic show of submission. Her attitude recalls Tacitus' reminder in the *Agricola* that under tyrants there are occasions when it is possible to pursue a middle course; to live a life in which honour and submission are combined; that those who choose this path often do a greater service than others who seek glory by a spectacular death.

Teresa lived in an age conspicuous for its violence and intolerance. When John of the Cross was imprisoned in Toledo by the Calced Carmelites who, with some justification, looked upon him as a rebel against his Order, he was whipped with such severity that his shoulders bore the scars for the rest of his life. These same Carmelites were regarded by Teresa as capable of having poison put into Padre Gracián's food—another reason why she liked him to have meals in the convents of the Discalced. Moreover Teresa herself, though renowned for her tenderness of heart towards all who were ill whether in body or mind, appeared to believe, nevertheless, that in dealing with neurotics a few blows 'well laid on' could occasionally be an effective remedy. She was a child of her century; to wrest her out of her context would be a distortion of the truth. No doubt she took certain things for granted that would repel people today. Yet, it is not unreasonable to see a touch of her characteristic irony in her choice of the 'Angels' and the 'Great Angel' as her pseudonyms for the Inquisitors and the Chief Inquisitor. What she felt about violence is hinted at in the *Way of Perfection*. Human strength, she says, cannot heal the ills of the day; force of arms has been tried and has failed. Is there, perhaps, a hint at the cynicism with which the Inquisitors handed over their prisoners to the state, when she says that help must come not from the secular arm but from the Church itself—from the lives and the prayers of those who are pleasing to God?

*   *   *

Travelling south from Valladolid, I broke my journey at the Escorial. It was May. There were chestnut trees outside my window, their pink blossoms showing among leaves that hung limp like half-opened umbrellas. Beyond the trees I saw the monastery of San Lorenzo; the blue lead roof, the spires and domes and cupolas; the balls, crosses and arrows—all glittering in the golden evening light. I had seen the Escorial earlier in the year on a day of drifting snow. It had looked forbidding then, like a prison. Now it was its elegance that impressed me. It had a dream-like quality, as though it had been let down from the sky in a net of gold. The long, pale walls were washed with gold. The window-panes were gold-leaf. The mountains, too, reflected gold, and had a strange translucency, as though they were visible one through another.

It was warm that night. Nobody seemed to go to bed. I could hear footsteps passing up and down, voices and laughter. The breeze scarcely stirred the chestnut leaves vividly green in the light of a street lamp. The monastery was an immense black pile against the stars. I cannot think of the Escorial without remembering the little chestnut trees, the contrast between their frail, transient beauty and the massive splendour of San Lorenzo, at once a monastery, a palace and a tomb. I remember them, too, in a storm, caught in the phosphorescent glow of lightning—the rain pattering on the leaves and the blossom scattered to the ground like fragments of coral.

I lay awake thinking of Teresa and Philip II. Never were two persons more different than the nun and the man who was her King. The one was natural, open-hearted, trusting, impetuous, gay; the other, inhibited, shut in upon himself, suspicious, cautious, morose. She called him 'our holy King' and 'my friend the King'. That was how she thought of him, how she saw him. It is unlikely that she realized that the autocratic Philip, while sincere in his desire to correct the abuses of his day by enforcing the decisions of the Council of Trent, was at the same time set upon bringing the religious Orders, by allowing them only Spanish Superiors, wholly in subjection to himself. Teresa's thoughts were centred on her Reform. For its success the friendship of the King was indispensable, and the best way to be sure of it was to assume it was hers already. Friendship, as Cicero has said, implies a certain equality—which explains the naturalness in her approach to Philip. She is not overawed by this man who holds life and death in his hands. In a letter sent to him through his sister the Infanta Juana, she writes the cryptic and daring words: 'Remember that Saul was anointed and yet he was rejected.' She prayed for him, too, with a particular solicitude and asked her nuns to do the same. He was a person, she said, who had passed through great trials and had more to come.

Her letters to him are deferential, yet not artificial. In one addressed to 'His Sacred Caesarian and Catholic Majesty', written from the Incarnation in June 1573, she begs him, after promising her poor prayers for himself, his Queen and his son, to give his protection to her Reform. In a longer one from Seville in July 1575 she asks that the Reform should be made into a separate province with Gracián as Superior: she has been among Carmelites for nearly forty years, so she should know what she is talking about. Then, after singing the praises of Gracián, she ends: 'For the love of God, I beg your Majesty to pardon me, for I see that I am being very bold.' In a third, longer still, written from Saint Joseph's in September 1577, she defends Gracián from attacks made upon both him and the houses of the Reform. The things that are being said about the Discalced would amuse her were it not for the harm they could do. Gracián, she reminds Philip, deserves better treatment. Apart from his good qualities, he comes of a family that has served the King well. In her excitement she adds a lengthy postscript, saying that the Discalced nuns are ready to swear for Gracián's character—a man so punctilious that he holds a Chapter from outside the convent grille—a procedure that no one else would consider necessary.

Then, there is the letter written in December of the same year, also from Saint Joseph's, in which, having begged forgiveness for her renewed boldness, she gives rein to her indignation against the Calced fathers—men who have no regard for justice or for God, with less compassion than the Moors. It is by these that John of the Cross is held a prisoner in such conditions that his life is in danger. She ends: 'Unless your Majesty gives orders that all this is put right, I don't know what is going to happen.'

Persons in the position of Philip live surrounded, if not by flatterers, at least by those whose words are trimmed. It is not surprising that he appreciated Teresa's simplicity and her sincerity. Whenever he read one of her letters, he was, Gracián has recorded, 'mightily pleased.' Nor is it surprising that he expressed a wish to see her. This was in Madrid as early as 1569, after she had sent him the letter through the Princess Juana. 'Can I not see this woman?' he is reputed to have exclaimed. But Teresa was already on her way to Toledo.

Did the two meet? Possibly not. On the other hand, at the Escorial I was told of a tradition that Teresa visited the King there somewhere between the years 1568 and 1573 and was given an audience in the room that is over the sacristy. I do not know what evidence there is for this. It would seem, however, to be borne out by a letter of doubtful authenticity addressed to Doña Inés Nieto and included in the collection of the Marqués de San Juan de Piedras Albas, published in 1915, in which the writer ('this poor woman') describes an interview with the King. His penetrating gaze made her lower her eyes, but when she looked a second time, his expression had become more gentle. When she knelt before him to thank him for his kindness, he bade her rise, gave her a courtly bow such as she had never seen before and held out his hand for her to kiss. The late Professor Allison Peers said that he found it easier to believe this letter was written by Teresa than by anyone else.

5

Toledo

Sᴏᴜᴛʜ of Madrid the landscape from the train was more gentle, more fertile than any I had yet seen. There was less rock, more trees, shrubs and flowers. There were acacias and tamarisks, and olives standing up from among poppies or trailing vines. White-walled farmsteads with pinky tiled roofs had gardens that were gay with marigolds and snapdragons and roses. The young corn was a brilliant golden green—the green in which El Greco clothes his saints. Plump cattle fed on land cut by criss-cross irrigation channels. A donkey with sacking covering its eyes was turning a water-wheel. Now and again a chalky hill tufted with grass rose abruptly. In the distance there were mountains. At Las Infantas I was delighted by terracotta wine jars standing on the platform, each one shapely and slender with two handles that stuck out like ears. As we drew nearer to Toledo the earth became a violent red; it swept up against the sky, like a tide of fire.

The station at Toledo is built of mulberry-coloured brick, in the Moorish style, with rounded arches and blue tiling let into the walls. A young man with American-cut clothes (he reminded me of the westernized Arabs I used to meet in Nazareth) darted at me, grabbed my case and heaved it on to his shoulder. *'Vamos!'* he said. That is the way to approach Toledo—on foot, leisurely. Not, indeed, that it was very leisurely, for the sun was hot and the *mozo* walked at a fine pace, talking unceasingly about the Damascene work that I must not fail to see, and then about the Civil War.

Ahead of me was the city, piled on its cliffs with a glorious dramatic carelessness. Below it the steel-glinting Tagus curved beneath the Alcántara bridge, between grim ash-grey boulders.

It was El Greco's Toledo; not as it appears in any specific painting, but an epitome of all the Toledo scenes that—sometimes
perhaps without the artist being aware of it—have slipped into
the background of his Christs and Virgins, martyrs and saints.
The sky was a deep ink-blue. Raindrops spattered. A silver
light breaking from the clouds washed towers and walls,
bridge and rocks, to that mysterious pallor that is the prelude to
a storm. It was El Greco's city, and El Greco's light; the light
that floods down upon Christ in Gethsemane and gives to the
face of the Count of Orgaz, as he is laid in the grave by the
Saints Augustine and Stephen, a strange, unearthly beauty.

The *Entierro del Conde de Orgaz* is in Santo Tomé, a church
with a tawny belfry that in sunlight has a sheen like silver,
standing at the corner of a street full of little shops selling needle-
work, Damascene brooches and knives, miniature bulls and
matadors. A crucifix with a lamp in front of it is built into the
outside wall, which is the same tawny stone as the belfry. I
used to sit in this church each day looking at El Greco's picture.
It was like a vision shining upon the darkness. Teresa never
saw it, for it was not commissioned until 1586, four years
after her death. However, she may well have seen other paintings of his. She was in Toledo, on and off, for four years from
June 1576. El Greco came to the city in the spring of 1577, and
shortly afterwards was working on the altar piece for the church
of Santo Domingo el Antiguo. He was commissioned, also, to
paint the *Espolio de Vestiduras* for the sacristy of the cathedral. A
picture of Saint Benedict and another of Saint Bernard belong
to this period too.

He must certainly have known of Teresa—if he did not meet
her or read her writings. Even before she founded the Toledo
convent in 1567, she was familiar in the city as the friend of
Doña Luisa de la Cerda. By 1577 she was a national figure; *la
Fundadora*, who had extended the Reform from Castile to
Andalusia and was supported, as was well known, by King
Philip himself.

El Greco and Teresa have much in common. Not because either, as far as we know, was consciously influenced by the other, but because each belongs to an age remarkable for its mysticism, whether genuine or false. The painter and the saint both reach out to a transcendental world seen in terms of colour and light. Teresa's descriptions of 'colours not seen in nature' and 'a radiance that does not dazzle' bring to mind the unearthly light and the ecstatic visions of El Greco's paintings.

In each of them, too, the natural and the supernatural are reconciled. Teresa is at home whether she is writing about business transactions, clergy, importunate relations, or conversations held with Christ and his saints. In the *Entierro del Conde de Orgaz* the elegant black-clothed *hidalgos* with their ruffs and their frills, their tapering hands and dark questioning eyes set in pale oval faces, are citizens of Toledo, persons known individually to the artist; but they are also citizens of the heavenly Jerusalem, with their gaze set on the glory of the Beatific vision. There is, however, a fundamental difference—possibly one of temperament—between El Greco and Teresa. The artist, who lived what is generally thought of as a worldly life, gives the impression, in his paintings, of one who is caught up to heaven. Teresa on the other hand, in spite of visions, raptures, even of levitation, remains for me someone whose feet are planted on this earth—in which respect she reminds me of those Thessalian witches who without themselves leaving the ground could bring down the moon on a golden thread.

*   *   *

The little mosque was shadowy and bronze-red, with horse-shoe arches one repeating the other, like an echo heard in the dusk. I felt that I had been transported into the world of the Moors. This was not wholly true. But I had not yet seen the faded Christian paintings on the walls above the arches, nor did I know that I was standing in what is called the Mesquita del Cristo de la Luz—so named because outside it, legend tells, the horse of the Cid suddenly knelt down, nor could it be prevailed upon to move until the wall was opened to reveal a figure of Christ in a niche lighted by lamps that the Goths had put there centuries earlier, in the church that existed before ever there was a mosque.

I was in a city where the centuries and civilizations meet and merge, yet do not lose their character. The Roman bridge is crowned with a Moorish gateway. The walls of the Synagoga del Tránsito are covered with that filigree moulding perfected by the Arabs, as intricate and delicate as the crochet with which my Edwardian aunts used to decorate their teacloths. In the Hospital de Santa Cruz, begun by Cardinal Mendoza and finished by Queen Isabella, the *mudéjar* ceilings look like the roof of a cave hung with stalactites, while in the cloisters below there are tombs bearing Hebrew inscriptions. In the Gothic cathedral Mass is celebrated each day in the Mosarabic rite that was followed by the Moorish converts to Christianity.

It is a city with an air of mystery. Its streets, ringing with the hooves of donkeys and the tap of the steel-worker's hammer, have beautiful, mysterious names. Calle de Niñas Hermosas (the street of the Beautiful Children). Calle de los Alfileres (the street of the Pins). Calle de Poso Amargo (the street of the Well of Bitterness). They are steep streets, many of them so narrow that the sky is no more than a shred of blue. Some shrink into a covered passage, called a *cobertizo*, that is lit, if lit at all, by a lamp in front of the shrine of some saint. It is mysterious, too, because it is very old. So old that no one can tell with certainty of its beginnings. Some say Hercules founded it. Others say it was the Jews, fleeing from Nebuchadnezzar— that they gave to it the name Toledoth, city of generations. The Romans called it Toletum, and made it the capital of the province of Carpetania. Among the rocks under the Alcázar there are the remains of an aqueduct, and outside the city a crescent-shaped enclosure known as the Circus Maximus. The Visigoths sacked the city and rebuilt it in their own tradition, imposing their architecture on that of the Romans and Christians. In the tenth century the Crusaders captured it from the Caliphs and set up their Gothic spires, turning mosques and synagogues into churches. Today, the bullet-scarred Alcázar is a witness to the life and death struggle of the Civil War.

In Teresa's day, Toledo was a place of some standing. The court was there until 1561, when Philip moved it to Madrid. Even after that the city continued for some time to be the home of many of the Spanish nobility. It was prosperous, and much frequented by merchants from abroad. Iron was forged, and steel for spears and swords was tempered in the waters of the Tagus. The slim Toledan blade was renowned for the strength and delicacy of its workmanship, and so flexible that it could be bent to make a complete circle. Shoes, too, were made, and brocades, velvets and taffetas. So were candles and tapers for churches. Its marzipan was as popular then as it is today. Persons coming from abroad liked the city's genial, cosmopolitan atmosphere; some who had come as visitors remained permanently.

We first hear of Teresa at Toledo in the spring of 1562, when she was sent to stay with Doña Luisa de la Cerda. During this visit, she moved among the grand ladies of the land, whom she treated not with an exaggerated deference but with the freedom of an equal. Far from being overawed by such persons, she felt compassion because of the cares and trials of their state. They are not even able, she says, to take their meals as they wish. The food they eat is regulated not by their constitution but their rank. What with this and jealousy among the servants, life as it is lived by the great is no better than slavery.

She was back five years later for the Malagón foundation; then again the following year, to found the Toledo convent. There was the usual trouble. The governor of the city was reluctant to give a licence, the councillors were in opposition. There was the difficulty, too, of finding a house. This was not solved, as one might have expected, through the influence of Doña

Luisa, but thanks to the help of a flashy-looking young gallant, called Andrada, who one morning when the nuns were at Mass in the Jesuit church turned up offering his services. His appearance caused some consternation and, still more, amusement. To judge by his clothes he was not at all the person for Discalced Carmelites to be seen talking to. Nevertheless, he was back the next day, a bunch of keys in his hand, to tell them that a house was at their disposal as soon as they cared to move in their furniture. This was a simple matter, since their household possessions amounted to two mattresses and a blanket.

I found Doña Luisa's house; a great derelict *palacio* facing on to a courtyard in which two little boys were fighting a duel with toy swords. A toothless old woman showed me a spacious downstairs room with a carved Moorish ceiling and blue tiles. There was a low window at which, she told me, *La Santa* used to sit sewing. We were joined presently by the woman's husband, who said that Teresa had visited this house as a girl, before becoming a nun. When I told him that I had not heard this before, he said that doubtless there were many things I had not heard. I could find no trace of the house provided by the young man, Andrada, which is believed to have been in the Plazuela de Barrio Nuevo, near the church of Santa María la Blanca, formerly a synagogue. The present convent, which goes back to 1608, was in Teresa's day the property of Doña Luisa's brother.

Toledo meant more to Teresa than any city in Spain, except possibly Ávila. It was her father's city (they called him *el Toledano*) and one in which she felt particularly at ease. She liked its genial atmosphere. The climate, too, suited her. 'I am better than I have been for years,' she tells Lorenzo in July 1576. The cold of Ávila was sometimes too much for her. While Prioress at the Incarnation she writes: 'Blessed be God, we shall have no changes of weather in eternity . . . I have found these parts so trying that you would never think that I had been born here. I don't think I have been well for as long

as six weeks together.' Then, having listed her complaints
which included quartan ague, a pain in the side, quinsy and
face-ache, she adds: 'It makes me laugh sometimes to think
that in spite of this I am able to do all the things I have to do.'
Toledo, too, could have extremes. In January 1577 the frost was
hardly less severe than at Ávila; but this was exceptional.
Moreover, in the Toledo convent she was particularly delighted by her cell, which was secluded, with a window looking on to the garden. It would have been perfect had it not been
for all the letters that she had to write. 'All these letters are
killing me,' she tells her brother. She says the same to Padre
Gracián, adding that to write a book (she was working on the
Foundations at the time) was far less exhausting.

Letters reveal the personality 'without powder or paint';
sine fuco ac fallaciis, as Cicero puts it. This is strikingly evident
in the case of Teresa who not only, as Gracián remarks,
governed her convents by letters but also wrote them to relatives, friends and acquaintances in every walk of life. The four
hundred and fifty available in English are only a fraction of the
whole. None are extant of those she wrote to Saint John of the
Cross, who is said to have carried them about with him in a
bag. According to one tradition, he destroyed them as an act
of self-abnegation. It is more likely that he did so to prevent
their falling into the hands of the Calced friars or others un-
friendly towards the Reform. Teresa frequently used pseudonyms to baffle persons who might read letters not meant for
them. She refers to Gracián as Eliseus or more often Paul, while
she herself is Ángela or Laurencia. The Calced Carmelites
are Egyptians or Owls; the Discalced, Butterflies; the Jesuits,
Ravens. Her letters wore her out, but for later generations they
have made her live. They reveal not only the Foundress with a
grasp on every detail of the Reform, the mystic able out of her
own experience to guide others in the spiritual life, but above
all a woman deeply human, caring intensely for others—someone moreover who is not above enjoying a gossip. 'I wish I

were with you,' she writes to her cousin María Bautista, the Prioress of Valladolid, who is suffering from depression, 'It would do you good to hear some entertaining chatter.' A little later she writes that after all it was as well she could not get to Valladolid, since the two of them would have lost so much sleep with their talking.

Teresa wrote letters far into the night by the light of an oil lamp, till her head ached. She used a quill pen and large sheets that when folded made pages about twelve inches by eight. She left an inch or so blank at the top and a margin on the left hand side. This was a convention required by good manners, but ignored by Peter of Alcántara who preferred, in the name of holy poverty, to use up every scrap of space. Teresa's holiness, on the other hand, never took the form of eccentricity, as is illustrated by the story of the partridge. 'There is a time for partridge, and a time for penance,' was her reply to an onlooker who was scandalized to see this 'saint' enjoying a well-cooked bird. At the beginning of a letter she put a large *I.H.S.*, at the end her signature. The day of the month or week was indicated by some such phrase as: 'Tomorrow will be Christmas Eve,' or, 'Yesterday was the feast of the Magdalene,' or, 'Today is Wednesday, just after twelve.' She had two seals; one bearing the device *I.H.S.*, the other a skull and cross-bones: *la Calavera*. In a letter to her brother Lorenzo she asks him to send her the former. 'I can't bear,' she says, 'sealing my correspondence with this death's head!' Again writing to her brother, she says: 'Don't bother to read over your letters to me. I never read over my own; if there are words missing, put them in and I will do the same for you; the thought can be seen at a glance.'

On his return from America, in 1575, Lorenzo eventually settled on an estate that he bought a few miles outside Ávila, called La Serna. After thirty years absence from his country he was glad to turn to his sister for advice. She suggests that he should have his kitchen 'partitioned off', so that he is not disturbed by the noise of the 'ploughboys'. Then, not wanting to

appear meddlesome, she adds: 'But how I chatter away!
After all, everyone knows his own house best.' She tells him
to buy himself a pony not a mule, but to let his two sons walk—
which they can well do. She is delighted that they are to be
educated in Ávila. With the Jesuits teaching grammar and
philosophy, and the Dominicans theology, there is no need
to go further afield—besides which, there is so much good
Christian living in the city that people coming from elsewhere
are amazed. The boys, she says, should be allowed to wear
college caps—a kind of hood called a *bonito* which was then
coming into fashion. They must be kept at their work, not
permitted to get into a 'stuck-up' set or use the title *don*, a
courtesy that meant more in sixteenth-century Spain than it
does today.

In her letters to her brother she thanks him repeatedly for
gifts: in particular for sweets, sardines and sea-bream—this
last was sent, when the weather was hot, between folds of
bread. In return she sends quinces for his housekeeper to make
into a preserve for him to have at dessert. Another time it is a
pot of jam which he is to eat himself, not give away; there is an
extra pot for the Sub-Prioress of Saint Joseph's, since Lorenzo,
'always a ladies' man' is a frequent visitor at the convent. She
also sends pastilles to be thrown into the brazier in his room.
'They are very healthy and purifying . . . excellent for colds
and headaches.'

She gives detailed instructions as to the wearing of a hair-
shirt which she has sent at his request. 'It makes me laugh,' she
writes, 'to think how you send me sweets and presents and
money and I send you hair-shirts.' He is to use it with discretion,
on no account to injure his health. 'During Lent you may wear
the hair-shirt one day every week on the understanding that,
if you find it does you harm, you take it off again.' A like discretion is to be observed in other pious practices. He is to have
at least six hours' sleep: 'Do not suppose that this blessing of
sound sleep which God gives you is an unimportant one.' And

again: 'Remember that we middle-aged people need to treat our bodies well, so as not to wreck the spirit.' Nor is he to be troubled at finding himself unable to pray: 'Don't imagine that it is always the devil who hinders prayer; sometimes the ability to pray is taken from us by the mercy of God. For many reasons that I have not the time to tell you, I would say that it is almost as great a mercy when he takes it away as when he gives it in full measure.' She mentions her own inability to pray, so pressed is she with work, then adds: 'I feel no scruples about this; I am merely sorry that I have not the time.' On one occasion Lorenzo took a notion that he ought to meditate on hell. 'Don't!' says Teresa.

She scolds him for making a vow without telling her 'I would not have dared to make such a vow!' 'I am sure God will have accepted your intention,' she goes on, 'but I think you would do better to change the nature of the vow.' The secret of the spiritual life, she says, is to flee from all to the All. But this is an attitude of mind, not a rule to be carried out to the letter. She is not impressed by Lorenzo's proposal to get rid of the carpets in his house, so as to live with greater austerity. Possessions are not important one way or another; it is attachment to them that is harmful. Nor must he think that he is not leading a spiritual life because he is busy attending to his property; it is right that he should look after the estate that will come down to his children. Jacob was not less pleasing to God because he was occupied with the care of his flocks.

Lorenzo's little daughter, the eight-year-old Teresita, spent some months at the Seville convent with her aunt. Teresa was delighted with her and so were the nuns. She wore a Carmelite habit and went about the house 'like a fairy', making everyone laugh with her tales of the Indians and the voyage home. When Teresa left for Malagón and Toledo, Teresita went too. She was in high spirits all the journey, and so excited by the time they reached Malagón that she could not eat her supper.

There was also in the Toledo convent Isabel Dantisco,

Gracián's little sister, a plump, pretty child. '*La mi Bella*,' Teresa calls her. She used to play with statues of the Christ child and Virgin and shepherds, make up poems and set them to music. One day when Teresa gave her a slice of melon, she complained that it 'deafened' her throat. Of the two children, Teresita was the more graceful, Bella the more intelligent. Bella had an ugly laugh, which was the more noticeable as she was always laughing. Teresa was kept busy trying to teach her to laugh prettily—she did this in private, so as not to embarrass the child.

Isabel's elder sister, Juana, was at a boarding school in Toledo; el Colegio de Doncellas Nobles. 'Really, from what she says, she has more trials to bear than we have!' Teresa comments. She did not like the idea of girls being herded together in large numbers and was against the suggestion that the nuns at Medina del Campo should run a school. 'As to taking all those girls, in the way you proposed,' she writes to a Jesuit, 'I have never liked the idea. I think that teaching young women and keeping them in order is as different from handling young men as black from white. . . . More than forty of them would be too many, and end in chaos. They would always be exciting one another. I know only too well,' she continues, 'what a lot of women are like, when they are all together. God defend us!'

The black sheep in Teresa's family was her brother Pedro, generally known as Pedro de Ahumada, (the one to whom she gave the *bolilla*), who had come back from America at the same time as Lorenzo. He was testy, querulous, a prey to fits of depression (he could not help himself, he used to say), with a grudge because his services to the King had not, he believed, been given adequate recognition. 'I ought to be moved by his distress,' Teresa writes, 'but I confess I feel most uncharitable towards him.' Nevertheless, she put herself out to help him and urged Lorenzo to do the same. It was not Pedro's moods that she minded but the fact that he was a worry to Lorenzo— in none too good health himself—who made his brother an allowance which he ran through almost at once, wandering restlessly from place to place. At one time it was suggested that Pedro should live in a monastery. Teresa put a stop to this. She pointed out that apart from anything else he would never stand the food. As it was, in the inn where he stayed at Toledo he used to send away the dishes that were set in front of him, complaining that they were not sufficiently spiced; he preferred to eat a bit of pie.

Few people, certainly few religious, have been as involved with their relatives as Teresa. It was not that she clung to them, but they to her. Her relatives, she used to say, wore her out. Fond as she was of Lorenzo, she admitted that she was relieved when he left Toledo for Ávila. Then there was her sister Juana, whose marriage was not an easy one. Teresa used to give her advice as to how to handle the hypersensitive and jealous Juan de Ovalle. In a letter to Lorenzo she calls her brother-in-law 'a perfect baby', yet begs him to be forbearing. The Ovalles were badly off. Lorenzo helped them financially and Teresa, whenever she was able, would send them 'some little thing'. She begs her sister not to be over-anxious; to remember that 'all things pass'. Above everything she is to love her, Teresa, not for any material help she may give (and the least said of this the better, since people talk), but because she remembers her always before God. Towards the end of her life Teresa was further drawn into the affairs of the Ovalles, when her niece, Beatriz, was involved in a scandal in Alba de Tormes. Because there had been gossip about the admiration shown her by a prominent citizen, who was already married, her parents, when the man became a widower, wanted to arrange a match between the two. Beatriz refused to marry him. Teresa had sympathy with her niece who, she felt, had been mishandled.

There were, also, Lorenzo's sons. Francisco, the elder, thought he would become a Carmelite in the monastery of the Reform at Pastrana. However, he had scarcely entered the novitiate when he came out again and married a girl of good family but penniless. The younger, a second Lorenzo, having renounced his inheritance at the age of eighteen, returned to America a month before his father's death, and made a good marriage there. He left behind him in Ávila an illegitimate daughter. In December 1581 Teresa writes to him: 'It was a great mercy of God that you fell on your feet so quickly. As you began to go your own way so young, you might have given us a lot of trouble. It makes me realize how fond I am of you, for though I am very grieved at your offence against God, the little girl is so like you that I can't help taking her to my heart and loving her dearly.' She goes on to tell him that, since the circumstances of the child's birth are not her fault, he must see that she is well brought up, and provided for. He should invest some money to be available when she needs it.

As well as brothers and sisters and their children, there were numerous relatives on the fringe of the family. One of these was the eccentric Ana de Cepeda, whom Teresa did not dare take into any of her convents: 'A curious character and not at all companionable.'

*　　*　　*

Touching on spiritual matters when writing to María de San José, the Prioress at Seville, Teresa shows the same discretion as in her letters to Lorenzo. Two slave girls who want to enter the Seville convent are not to be discouraged by 'talk about "perfection" '; if they do well what is essential, that is enough. With regard to a convent at Paterna where reforms are being introduced (Teresa was not reforming the convent but had been consulted), too much, she says, must not be expected of the nuns: to impose a rigid silence or other rules to which they are not used would be to force them into committing offences they would not otherwise have thought of; those in authority should treat the sisters gently, leaving the rest to God. In no convent are excessive and foolish mortifications to be allowed.

The Prioress at Malagón had said, it appears, that one nun might give another 'a sudden blow'. 'On no account,' Teresa writes, 'must you ever order or allow any nun to strike another —and that applies to pinching too—or bring up your nuns with the severity that you saw practised at Malagón. They are not slaves, and the only reason for practising mortification is that they should profit from it. I tell you, my daughter, you need to look very carefully at the kind of things that inexperienced prioresses take it into their heads to do; they cause me the greatest distress.' The habit of pinching was one that had come down from the days of the Incarnation. Teresa's sound sense and understanding of human nature is shown again in the advice she gives María de San José concerning the approaching visit of some Jesuit fathers: 'You must let them have their own way, for though we may not always like what they say, it is so important for us to have their help that it is best to conform with their wishes. Think out questions to ask them, for that is what they like.'

The deep affection she felt for María de San José did not blind Teresa to her friend's faults. She complains to Gracián oe the 'childish goings on' of the Prioress of Seville; also, that she is more shrewd than befits her vocation. She tells her in one letter that she is a 'fox', *raposa;* presumably in reference to onf of the numerous business transactions of which mention is made—the selling of securities; the matter of dowries; the payment of rent and in particular a property tax levied on the Seville convent, called an *alcabala*, for which Lorenzo provided an advance. More often, however, Teresa is thanking her for gifts: orange water, oil of orange, sweets, potatoes, spices, dogfish, tunny. 'The tunny fish,' she says in one letter, 'was left at Malagón, and long may it stay there!' quinces, 'seven lemons', coconuts. 'The sisters are delighted to see the coconuts and so was I. Blessed be he who created them!' When she wants something she asks for it. On one occasion it is orange petals preserved in sugar—a few will do but they must be 'in sugar'.

Another time, it is a 'large *Agnus Dei* and two emerald rings' belonging to Teresita.

Teresa used to say that, for her, gratitude was no virtue, since she could be bribed by the gift of a sardine. One of the earliest letters written from Toledo is to a certain Doña Juana de Lobera, thanking her for a book on surgery written by her father—it is thought to have been *The Treatise on the Four Courtly Ailments*, by John Luis de Lobera Dávila, physician to Charles V—which Teresa had wanted as a present for a medical friend and benefactor. In the letters to María de San José she says repeatedly that she wishes she could make an adequate return for the kindnesses shown to her: 'I should like more than anything,' she writes, 'to repay you in some degree for what you send. After all, such things are a mark of affection.' Fond as she is of Toledo, she is exasperated when she cannot get some material that she wants to send to a friend. 'Never in my life,' she says, 'have I seen a place so barren in anything to do with taste.'

*   *   *

It was in the peace of her cell at Toledo that Teresa began the *Interior Castle*. In colour, richness and variety this greatest of her writings may be compared to a symphony in which the theme is the journey of the soul to God. Taking the image of the castle made from a single diamond illuminated from within, she traces the soul's progress from the outer court, where there are reptiles and other venomous creatures, through room after room (the book's original title was *Las Morades*, the equivalent of the Bible mansions) until it reaches the chamber of the King in the centre. It is a journey in prayer and, therefore, in love, detachment and humility—the journey of any soul, but particularly her own. In a letter to María de San José she asks her to read part of what she has written to Baltasar Álvarez, her former confessor. 'Read him,' she says, 'the last Mansion and tell him that the person has reached that stage and attained the peace that belongs there.'

It could be thought of, too, as a meditation on the purpose of the Carmelite life as set out in the *Liber Primorum Monachorum*, a book familiar to the religious of Teresa's time: a purpose that is twofold—at once a giving and a receiving. The soul that gives itself to God will find within itself the solace and strength of God's presence—this latter, a gift given by God himself, *ex mero Dei dono*, beyond the reach of human strivings.

It is characteristic of Teresa that, having chosen the allegory of the castle, she refuses to be restricted by it. As in her other writings, she takes her imagery from where she will. Thinking of the Castilian shepherd piping to his flock, she says that the soul on its journey, if it is patient and resolute, will hear, when least thinking to hear it, the note of the Good Shepherd calling gently. Then, its own efforts are no longer needed. It has only to follow. God will do all. The water (her images are piled one upon another) springs up now from the source, filling the fountain basin—flooding the soul. *Dilatasti cor meum*, as the psalmist says. If the soul is consenting, like wax that waits the imprint of the seal, love shall be united with Love. And the purpose of this union? Again, she turns to the psalmist. 'If, as David says, with the Holy we shall be holy, then assuredly, being made one with the Strong, we shall win strength through this sovereign union of spirit with Spirit.' The soul with strength renewed is to come to the help of all who are in the castle, that they in turn may accomplish their task whether great or small; 'for the Lord does not look at the magnitude of what we do, but at the love with which we do it.'

Her book ended, Teresa thinks of her nuns. In what reads more like a postscript to a letter than a formal epilogue, she urges that, being cloistered and with few diversions, they should take their pleasure in this spacious castle where they are free to wander at will. If any one of them thinks that she cannot go beyond the first rooms, she is not to be discouraged nor force herself to go further. It may be that she who feels unfit to enter the third room will find herself welcomed by Christ into the fifth and so from room to room. Even if the Prioress calls her away, she is not to be troubled: the Lord will keep the door open against her return.

The writing of the *Interior Castle* cannot have taken more than three months. Teresa began it on Trinity Sunday (June 2nd) 1577, worked at it probably continuously for a month or six weeks, then hardly touched it until well on in October. She finished it on the Vigil of Saint Andrew (November 30) at Saint Joseph's, Ávila.

The suggestion to write it had come, in the first instance, from Gracián, when she was expressing regret one day that the *Life* was in the hands of the Inquisition. Could she not, he said, write another book, giving her thoughts on prayer more fully? She was hesitant. She objected that there were too many books on prayer already. Besides, it was a task for learned men: she had neither the health nor the wits, and would be better left to her spinning. In the foreword she compares herself to a bird that can only repeat mechanically the notes that it has been taught.

The happenings of the year 1577 were not of a kind conducive to the writing of a book. She had written as far as the second chapter of the fifth Mansion when she had to leave Toledo for Ávila in the middle of July to arrange for the transference of the convent of Saint Joseph from the jurisdiction of the Bishop to that of the Carmelite Order. This had not been long settled when she learnt that Felipe Sega, a scholar and a man of upright character but violently prejudiced against the Reform, had arrived in Madrid as Papal Nuncio. His indictment of Teresa is well known. He calls her a *fémina inquieta, andariega, desobediente y contumaz*; 'a restless, disobedient and contumacious gad-about who under the cloak of piety has invented false doctrines, left the enclosure of her convent

against the orders of the Council of Trent and her own Superiors and gone about teaching as though she were a professor
(*como maestra*) contrary to the injunctions of Saint Paul who
said that women were not to teach.' Gracián, too, the Superior
of the Discalced was in disrepute; in the middle of September
she was writing to Philip pleading on behalf of 'this servant of
God'. As if this were not enough, in October there was turmoil
in the Incarnation when nuns who voted for Teresa to be
Prioress were excommunicated by the Provincial of the Calced
Carmelites; he was so angry that he 'pounded the voting papers
with his fist,' then burnt them.

In addition, she was suffering from severe headaches as
well as noises in her head. In the fourth chapter of the *Interior
Castle* she writes: 'My head sounds as if it were full of brim-
ming rivers, and then as if all the water in those rivers came
suddenly rushing down. A host of little birds, too, seem to be
whistling, not in my ears, but in the upper part of the head
where the higher part of the soul is said to be.' 'Yet,' she adds,
'the tranquillity and love in my soul are unaffected.' Despite
all, the book was finished and she knew it was good. Comparing it to the *Life* she says: 'It is composed of finer enamel and
more precious metals; the goldsmith was not so skilful when
he made the first.'

6

Pastrana, Segovia, Salamanca

ALCALÁ DE HENARES is the birthplace of Cervantes. It is a medieval town about twenty miles from Madrid, with pinkish stone walls, a long straggling street, arcades, university buildings with shabby plateresque façades, churches and two Carmelite convents. From it a road twists, mile after mile, through barren country. I had been lulled almost to a stupor by the monotony of tawny earth and glaring sun when suddenly I saw Pastrana below me, closed about by the hills. The ancient tiled roofs, cinnamon-coloured, black and mottled, on different levels, at different angles, seemed to overlap one another, like the plates on the shell of a tortoise.

It was the *siesta* hour. There was not a sound, not a movement in the deserted streets, some of them so steep and so littered with stones that to go along them was like stepping on the dried-up course of a mountain torrent. It was silent, too, in the *plaza*. The sun beat down on the stone cross and the dusty acacia trees. Under a colonnade supported by wooden pillars some men sat drinking. No one spoke. A mule laden with immense sacks was tethered nearby, its head drooping. Facing me I saw a renaissance gateway with classical pillars and over it a coat of arms framed in a pediment. It was the entrance to the Éboli palace, once the home of the eccentric, one-eyed Ana de Mendoza y la Cerda, Princess of Éboli and wife of the Portuguese Ruy Gómez de Silva, Philip's adviser and favourite, a man known for his discretion, of whom it was said that he rarely spoke and then only at the appropriate time. Inside, in a forecourt, some covered mule-carts stood with shafts uptilted. Beyond this was the main courtyard, enclosed by walls in which the windows were as blank as eye-sockets in a skull. Broken shutters hung from some of them.

I crossed the courtyard and pushed open a heavy door. There was no one to question me, no one to interfere. Inside, the vast, dark rooms were neglected and desolate. A carpenter's bench stood in one and the floor was strewn with wood-shavings. Cobwebs hung from carved and painted ceilings. Fireplaces and walls were blackened with smoke. I went up a shadowy staircase, then from one lonely room into another. A bat flittered out of darkness, almost brushing my face.

The Princess used to come here from her palace in Madrid when she was bored with the social round or exhausted with the sultry heat of the city. She watched her husband, fifteen years older than herself, with respect but with little under-standing as he devoted himself with a determination that was almost fanatical to the improvement of Pastrana. He settled a colony of Moriscos, descendants of those who had been driven out of Granada, to teach improved methods of farming and irrigation—in particular the cultivation of the mulberry. He brought silk-weavers and weavers of tapestry, silversmiths and goldsmiths.

Ana de Mendoza lived on here after her husband's death. Philip used to visit her, travelling the long lonely road from Alcalá de Henares by which I had come that morning. Antonio Pérez, the King's secretary, came too. In her husband's life-time the elegant dashing Pérez had been as a son to herself and to Ruy Gómez. Some say that in these later years he became her lover. At any rate, the two were involved in a political murder, with the result that the Princess was confined by order of Philip, first in the grim Torre de Pinto, that you can see from the train as you go south from Madrid, then in the Castle of Santorcaz, in Castile, and finally in her own home in Pastrana where she spent the last thirteen years of her life a prisoner behind bars.

A door with heavy bolts opened into a room that was smaller

than the others. There was an easel standing in it, and some canvases resting against the walls. One was an unfinished painting of a young woman with a striking, elongated face, dark hair piled high and a black patch covering the right eye. She wore drop ear-rings and a dress of sprigged brocade.

I had turned away from the painting and was looking out of the window. Iron bars criss-crossing against dazzling sunlight made me feel slightly dizzy. I could see the *plaza*, white and dusty and, beyond, olive trees metallic grey against the hills, and further still, mountains.

It was then I heard the footsteps. I felt panic. The loneliness weighed upon me. I wanted to escape, but the only way was the one by which I had come, and it was from there the noise came. I heard it again, footsteps coming closer. Then, in the doorway, I saw a young man with black tousled hair and strange pale eyes, like the eyes of a goat. 'The Princess was a prisoner in this room. She died in this room!' he said. He spoke the words in Spanish, dramatically—as though he were a herald making a proclamation. Then he turned and went.

It is easy, as a rule, to think of the great ones of the world as dead, perhaps because even in life they are already remote from most of us; kings and queens, warriors, statesmen and men of letters. It is easy to imagine them in shadowy Elysian fields with others of their kind, moving through meadows of asphodel. But I could not fit the Princess of Éboli into such a picture. There was nothing remote about her. She was all too human with her whims and her tantrums. I could not think of her as dead. I could not even think of the sufferings of her last years—the days and nights of loneliness and illness passed in this room in a confinement that was shared by her daughter. I could think of her only as someone faintly comic, who had brought chaos into Teresa's convent at Pastrana.

The Pastrana convent was founded in July 1569. Teresa had settled into the Toledo house barely a fortnight—she was worn out with consultations with workmen—when one morning as she was sitting down to a meal in the refectory, thinking to herself that she would have some rest during the approaching feast of Pentecost, a servant of the Princess of Éboli arrived with an imperious message to come at once to Pastrana to make a foundation there. Teresa's first reaction was not to go: she even spent some time (while the servant was given a meal) composing a letter to the Princess to that effect. Then, after praying before the Blessed Sacrament and consultations with her confessor, she changed her mind. It would have been unwise to offend Ana de Mendoza. Her husband had influence with the King.

In fact, two houses were founded. One for friars, one for nuns. Among the first friars were two Italians whom Teresa had met in Madrid when she broke her journey at the house of Doña Leonor de Mascareñas on the way to Pastrana. One of these was Juan de la Miseria, an artist who later painted her portrait at Seville. The other was Mariano Azaro, better known as Mariano de San Benito, a Neapolitan doctor of some distinction, as well as a soldier and an engineer. After serving in the army of the King of Poland and taking part in the battle of Saint Quentin, he was employed by Philip on schemes to make the Guadalquivir navigable from Seville to Córdoba and to use the Tagus for the irrigation of the country round Aranjuez. In the story of the Reform he stands out as a person of gifts but an excitable and over-hasty disposition.

The monastery at Pastrana was founded with no great difficulty. With the convent it was otherwise. The Princess of Éboli had her own ideas. When these went contrary to the Carmelite rule, Teresa, who was generally ready to make a compromise, refused to give in; she was prepared to go away rather than do so. Had it not been for the tact and reasonableness of Ruy Gómez, who persuaded his wife to modify her demands, there would have been no convent. It used to be said of Ruy that he covered a thousand of his wife's misdemeanours. When Ruy Gómez died in July 1573, the grief of the Princess knew no bounds. Nothing would satisfy her except that she should there and then become a nun in the Pastrana convent. According to one account, she bullied the unwilling Mariano into giving her the habit in her husband's death chamber. At any rate, she drove up to the convent that day, with her luggage and two ladies' maids. 'The Princess a nun!' the Prioress exclaimed. 'Then, the convent is finished.' She was right. For a couple of days the new sister—she had taken the name Ana de la Madre de Dios—behaved with an exaggerated meekness. After that, she began to show herself in her true colours. She expected the nuns to treat her with the deference due to one of her rank, even to the extent of waiting on her upon their knees. Nor would she accept any restriction of her liberty; she expected to receive visitors when she chose, along with their retinue of retainers. When she could not have her way, she retired to a hermitage at the end of the garden and had a door made in the wall through which she could communicate freely with the outside world. Finally, through the intervention of Philip, who told her that it was her duty to attend to her property and numerous children, she returned to her palace. Even so she continued to interfere in the affairs of the Discalced, plaguing the nuns to such a degree that their lives were a misery. Eventually, Teresa arranged that Julián de Ávila should remove them to the convent that she had founded at Segovia. She warned them to leave behind anything that the Princess had given. It was a wise precaution, for they had scarcely settled into their new home when they heard that they were threatened with a law-suit.

The party left Pastrana at dead of night, the nuns walking in procession to the top of a hill outside the town, where five mule waggons were waiting. 'We felt,' Julián de Ávila writes, 'like David as he retreated barefoot with his troops from before Absalom.' On the following day there was trouble crossing a river. The muleteers, instead of going to the ferry, had decided to cross by a ford. The waggons had scarcely entered the water in single file when those in front were caught in a current. The mules stopped dead, refusing to go either backwards or forwards. There was a fine uproar—Julián de Ávila shouting at the muleteers, the muleteers at the animals, the nuns at God.

*   *   *

Segovia on a morning in August. The countryside was flooded with a golden light such as I have seen before only on the foothills about Jerusalem. There was golden corn too, still unharvested, and the tarnished gold of stubble. Cocks were crowing. Like Ávila, Segovia stands high on the mountains, but it is a gentler city; less austere, less martial in character. The cathedral's lantern tower looked as if it was made out of wax from the honeycomb. The Alcázar was like a ship riding the sky. Yet it is not so much the cathedral or the Alcázar that bring visitors to Segovia; nor the ancient streets with their lopsided timbered houses; nor even the taverns where they serve sucking pig and trout wrapped in slices of ham. The 'attraction' of Segovia is the aqueduct. People come from all over the world to stare at it in admiration; at the immense elongated arches standing a hundred feet from the ground, built of cyclopean slabs of granite laid one on top of another with no mortar to hold them together. I thought it was like some horrible monster bestriding roofs and spires and streets, pedestrians, mule-carts and buses; flinging its evil shadow over city and countryside. It is said to have been constructed in Trajan's reign by one Licinius. I prefer to believe the story that Satan built it overnight.

Teresa's convent is at the corner of a street, almost in the shadow of the cathedral. In a letter to her friend Don Antonio Gaytán of Alba de Tormes, who accompanied her on several of her journeys, she calls it a 'very good house' and describes its position exactly: 'near Saint Francis in the Calle Real in the best residential district near the market place'. I am left with a

vivid impression of this convent; the little figures of Saint
Joseph and the boy Jesus carved under Teresa's direction high
up on the street wall; the dark porch with the low timbered
ceiling; the white-walled *locutorio*; the nuns slipping me pictures of Saint John of the Cross between the bars of the grille
and urging me to visit his tomb in the Discalced monastery on
the outskirts of the city. I was amazed, when I saw the tomb,
that such a pile of marble should honour a saint so small in
stature, so great in poverty.

It was in the *locutorio* of the Segovia convent that Gracián
and the Dominican theologian, Diego de Yanguas, met in
Teresa's presence to discuss the manuscript of the *Interior
Castle*. Gracián has described these meetings: 'I would take
up various phrases in the book, saying that they did not sound
well to me, and Fray Diego would reply, while she would tell
us to delete them. We did delete a few, not because there was
any erroneous teaching in them, but because many persons
would find them too difficult to understand; for such was the
depth of my affection for her that I wanted to make sure that
there should be nothing in her writings that might cause
anyone to stumble.'

But I am running ahead in Teresa's story. This incident
occurred in the summer of 1580. It was in March 1574, on the
feast of Saint Joseph, that she first came to Segovia, accompanied by John of the Cross and Julián de Ávila. There was an
uproar because she had not brought a written authority to
make a foundation—there was only a verbal permission given
on her behalf to a friend. The Vicar General arrived on the
scene in a towering rage that frightened Julián de Ávila so
much that he hid behind a staircase, leaving John of the Cross
to bear the brunt. Eventually peace was restored, but only after
John had been threatened with imprisonment and an officer
of the law stationed at the door.

*   *   *

Salamanca at nightfall is a scene set for *Carmen*. Buildings burnished like copper, ornately carved and aglow with lights, loom out of the shadows, as though piled one upon another. Lights glitter along tree-lined streets. The great, arched Plaza Mayor is flooded with light.

But Salamanca is always beautiful. I remember it after rain; the sun breaking through tattered clouds, picking out each shell on the Casa de las Conchas, turning the façade of the university to beaten gold. I remember it, too, in the dawn; the twin domes of the Old Cathedral black against the sky; poplar trees ghost-like at the river's edge; the 'tink' of an Angelus bell, faint yet insistent, refusing to be drowned by louder, deep-toned bells. Women with baskets of carnations used to pass below the window. Later, I would hear the desolate cry of a blind man selling lottery tickets.

Within a stone's throw of where I stayed was the Palacio Monterrey. Great chains hang at the entrance commemorating a royal visit. Teresa mentions the palace in a letter to her friend Doña Catalina Dávila: 'I must tell you how delighted her ladyship, the Countess of Monterrey, was to read your letter and to have news of you. . . . We are staying near her palace. So, if we need anything, it will be perfectly simple to see her. One of her servants brought me the money and a generous gift, so we are greatly indebted both to her Ladyship, your noble relative, and yourself.' This was in October 1573, when Teresa had come to the city to move her nuns into a new house. She refers to the same occasion in the *Foundations* where she writes: 'We were helped a great deal by the Countess of Monterrey, Doña María Pimental.' Some two years earlier after making a foundation at Alba de Tormes she had spent a few days at the palace with the Count and Countess before returning to Ávila.

Teresa founded the Salamanca convent in November 1570—after that of Pastrana, but over three years before the one at Segovia. She arrived from Ávila on the eve of All Saints

accompanied by María del Sacramento, an elderly nun from
the Incarnation. The city's intellectual life was at its zenith then.
Students rich and poor came from all over Spain and the outside world as well. In 1546 there were over five thousand, in the
eighties nearly seven thousand. To this day the room in which
Luis de León used to lecture remains as it was: the high small
windows, the Gothic pulpit, the rough benches, the clumsy
wooden desks scored with names.

The house that had been taken for the nuns was previously
occupied by students, who vacated it unwillingly, leaving a
fine mess behind them. On the first night Teresa and her companion were alone. María del Sacramento could not get the
students out of her mind; she imagined that some of them
might still be in hiding. Even when the two of them had bolted
themselves into the room she was still not at ease. She kept
peering round. Teresa asked her what was the matter. 'I was
wondering,' she said, 'what you would do all by yourself if I
were to die here.' The lugubrious suggestion, along with the
tolling of the church bells—for it was the vigil of All Souls—
did unnerve Teresa a little; for though she was not afraid of
corpses, the sight of them upset her. However, she took herself
in hand. 'Well,' she answered, 'I'll think about that when the
occasion arises. Meanwhile let me go to sleep.'

The house where this happened is in a small *plaza* that takes
its name from the Saint. It is a school for orphans now, run by
Las Siervas de San José. The little *patio* with the cream-coloured
pillars, the fig tree and the well, go back to Teresa's day. So
does the wooden staircase leading up to the room which was
hers for many months. It was in this *patio*, they tell you, that
she went into an ecstasy during recreation on Easter Sunday
1571, while a novice, Isabel de Jesús, was singing a couplet on
the theme of eternal life.

The episode on the vigil of All Souls is described in the
Foundations which Teresa began to write while she was in
Salamanca—not on this occasion, but when she came back to

move the convent. She wrote the first nine chapters, then broke off for the time being on account of 'numerous occupations'. This book, as well as being the story of the Reform together with digressions on prayer, revelations and the handling of neurotic nuns, is a commentary on the life of the times as valuable as *Pepys's Diary*. An instance of this is the account of the foundation at Alba de Tormes, made from Salamanca at the request of Francisco de Velásquez, steward of the Duke of Alba, and his wife Teresa de Layz. The latter, who belonged to a noble family, was as a child so little wanted by her parents, because she was a girl, that on the third day after her birth they left her entirely alone and neglected. In spite of this she survived, but not unnaturally grew up in a state of opposition to her mother and father, with the result that when they said it was time for her to marry she refused. However, on being introduced to the man who had been chosen for her husband, she changed her mind. Apart from the fact that there were no children, the marriage was a happy one. She was a devoted wife, while her husband wanted only to please her. When, therefore, to help fill the gap caused by their childless state, she suggested, in accordance with a custom of the times, that they should found a convent of contemplative nuns, he was glad to fall in with her proposal.

Alba de Tormes, however, is memorable not for Teresa de Layz but because it was there that Teresa of Ávila died. Those who like relics can see the Saint's heart in a vase decorated with rings presented by the devout, also her forearm preserved in a crystal tube mounted in gold and set with precious stones. I preferred to contemplate the tower of the Duke of Alba's castle standing alone against the sky—all that remains (the castle itself was destroyed in the Peninsular War) of a mansion once the most splendid in Spain, enriched by the spoils of conquered peoples, adorned by painters and sculptors, the scene of poetic and musical contests; renowned, too, for the beauty of its gardens. Teresa, when she stayed there in January

1574, was astounded by the treasures that were displayed in one room alone; china and glass and all manner of rare objects set out in such a way that she saw them at a glance as she came in. I was to be reminded of her experience when I visited a duchess in Andalusia who had collected into a tiny house all that had been salvaged from her mansion devastated in the Civil War. Every wall was covered with pictures; every table and shelf crammed with china, crystal, jade, crucifixes, little dressed figures of the saints, ornaments of silver and gold. There were, besides, cages of love-birds, several cats and in the bathroom tortoises.

7

Córdoba, Seville

I HOPE that one day I shall visit Córdoba again. I was in it scarcely longer than Teresa when she broke her journey there on the way from Beas to Seville. This has the advantage that, as I had no wish to see the modern industrial city, there is nothing to blur the picture I have carried away of a Córdoba mainly Moorish—a city of rounded arches; of quiet streets flanked by white-walled houses; great nail-studded doors; windows enclosed in grilles; balconies topped with brass balls; cascading flowers and greenery; wrought iron gateways opening into pillared courtyards beautiful with palms and lemon trees and cool with the splash of fountains. I remember an alley between walls hung with pots of trailing ferns—and overhead a strip of sky startlingly blue between picot-edgings of gold-red pantiles—winding under an arch past a faded painting of the Virgin, then ending in a dazzle of sunlight in a *plaza* where a crucifix, carved in stone, rose from a cluster of lamps each supported on a black iron stem that twisted weirdly.

Making my way through white cobbled streets, I came upon the Carmelite convent founded seven years after Teresa's death. Over the 'turn' a skull and crossbones was set into the plaster on the wall. There was a cool white-walled chapel, and a *patio* with red roses blooming against a white archway. A tiny child with dark solemn eyes was watering an aspidistra. The spray made a hissing, sleepy sound.

From the convent I went on in the direction of the river. The heat seemed to rise up from the pavement in waves. On my left were golden-yellow crenellated walls, then a gateway into a courtyard laid out with orange trees and palms in front of the Great Mosque. It was cool, almost cold in the mosque. The pillars supporting the horse-shoe arches gave the impression of a forest of exotic coral-coloured trees with black and white markings reaching away into an unending, shadowy distance. I knew that in this mosque, enclosed within its walls, there was a Baroque cathedral, yet I had no inclination to see it. I was enchanted by the strange, coral-coloured trees.

I went out into the heat and the glare and continued down to the pillared Puerta del Puente leading on to the Roman bridge that was restored in the time of the Moors, then enlarged by Philip II. Below it the Guadalquivir, shrunk by the summer drought, slid almost imperceptibly between pale parched banks. On the far side I saw the turreted mass of the Torre de la Calahorra, and, beyond, the sandy and white houses on the Campo de la Verdad; then, more distant still, the rolling, lion-coloured countryside.

Teresa, with Julián de Ávila and a small company of nuns, came to this bridge early on a Sunday morning in May 1578. They had decided to hear Mass in the church on the Campo de la Verdad, thinking to draw less attention to themselves than if they went to one of the city churches. Their hopes were dashed. To take their cart across the bridge a permit was needed from the governor of the town: *el corregidor*. It took them two hours to get this, because the persons concerned were not out of bed. Meanwhile, a staring crowd had gathered—not that they could see much, since the carts were entirely covered over. Then, when the permit was at last obtained, the vehicle could not get through the gate at the end of the bridge until pieces of wood had been sawn off either axle.

When the party eventually reached the church they were dismayed to find that, as it was dedicated to the Holy Spirit and this was Whitsunday, an exceptionally large congregation had gathered for the High Mass and sermon which were to be followed by a procession and dancing. Teresa felt they would have been justified in continuing on their way without hearing Mass.

Julián de Ávila, however, had scruples; it was advisable, he said, not to burden their consciences unnecessarily. As he was the theologian, the others felt bound to give in. The appearance in the church of these strange-looking nuns with their white cloaks and hemp-soled sandals caused, Teresa says, as much stir as if a herd of bulls had been let loose. Mercifully a kind-hearted *caballero* showed them into a side chapel and remained there with them.

I was reading a tablet on the wall of the church recording Teresa's visit, when I was joined by a bearded artist, an Englishman whom I had met in Madrid. We went into a little tavern with great wooden tubs in it and a smell of garlic, and drank *cerveza*. Through the open door I could see the dust rising in little tawny twirls, then subsiding. My companion asked me about Teresa. The name was vaguely associated in his mind with Lisieux and showers of roses. I told him a little about the Spanish Teresa and her misadventures at Córdoba, and how, when she and her companions came out of the church, they took their *siesta* a few minutes away under the Roman bridge, after chasing away some pigs.

Their journey from Beas had been a trying one. When they left soon after Easter the heat had been so violent that the provisions which had been meant to last for some days, had immediately gone bad. Water was scarce, and more costly than wine. It was a clammy, oppressive heat, far different from that of Castile. The sun beat down on the roofs of the carts so that to go into them was like entering purgatory. To pass the time the nuns tried to meditate on the fires of hell. Teresa became ill with fever, yet her spirit did not desert her. She used to tell stories and make up couplets to amuse the others. She was delighted by the birds and flowers in a glade in which they rested.

Apart from the fright they had when a boat taking one of the carriages across the Guadalquivir was swept away by a current, there were also the appalling inns. At one they were given a room roofed like a shed, with no window and the sun streaming in each time the door was opened. A bed was provided for Teresa, because she was ill, but it felt as though it were filled with sharp stones. Added to this there were vermin, men swearing and fighting—to say nothing of the din of music and dancing which 'neither entreaties nor gifts could quell'. They found it preferable to camp out of doors.

The General of the Carmelite Order had forbidden the founding of religious houses in Andalusia. When Teresa founded the convent at Beas in February 1575, she did not know that the town was in Andalusia; 'I should tell you,' she writes to María Bautista, 'that Beas is not in Andalusia, but five leagues this side of it; I am well aware I must not make any foundations in Andalusia.' However, when she went on to Seville, she knew what she was doing. It was a matter of divided loyalties. She went at the instigation of Gracián, whose authority as Apostolic Visitor to Andalusia—a position delegated to him by a Dominican, called Francisco de Vargas, who had been appointed by the Holy See—she considered superior to that of the General. In a letter to Inés de Jesús, Prioress of Medina del Campo, written from Beas in May 1575, in which Teresa says she is not looking forward to a summer spent in the grilling heat of Seville, she goes on: 'It appears, after all, that this house is in Andalusia and as Fray Master Gracián is Provincial of Andalusia, [she meant Apostolic Visitor] I found that I was subject to his authority without knowing it, and that being so, he has the power to command.' It was a power that she submitted to willingly. After her first meeting with Gracián she made a vow of obedience to him. She took this vow at Pentecost, she explains in the *Spiritual Relations*, in a hermitage at Écija, a Moorish town between Córdoba and Seville. She made the reservation that the vow was to apply only to matters not contrary to the will of God, or superiors to whom she already owed obedience. Moreover, it was to relate only to serious affairs; she would not, for example, be breaking it if she wished to importune Gracián about something which he had told her not to refer to again! On the other hand, she would not knowingly conceal from him any of her faults or sins.

Her first meeting with Gracián had taken place at Beas. In the letter to Inés de Jesús that I have mentioned above, she writes: 'Mother, how much I have wished you were with me these last few days. I must tell you that without exaggeration I think that they have been the best in my life. For over three weeks we have had Fray Master Gracián here, and much as I have had to do with him I assure you I have not yet realized his worth. To me he is perfect—and for our needs better than anyone we could have asked God to send us.' She begs Inés and her nuns to pray that he shall become Superior of the Discalced. 'If that happens,' she goes on, 'I can have a rest from governing these houses, for anyone so perfect and so gentle I have never seen.'

This was the beginning of a friendship that was to last till her death. At the time of their meeting at Beas, Gracián was thirty years of age, of high birth, Polish on his mother's side, exceptionally gifted and with great charm. Teresa was sixty. She calls herself *una vejezuela*: a little old woman. Gracián had joined the Reform at Pastrana in April 1572, taking the name Jerónimo de la Madre de Dios. Less than four months after his profession he was Apostolic Visitor in Andalusia. This was the man who was to be the first Discalced Provincial; who, in the history of the Reform, was to be judged by some a fool, by others a weakling, by others a saint.

*   *   *

To go from Castile to Andalusia is to travel, on the map, from north to south; to leave behind the stern Gredos mountains and the plain; to pass through the windmill country of Don Quixote where the earth is paler than in Castile and the walls of farms are white. It is also to pass, gradually, from a world

that is relatively western—though less so than anywhere north
of the Pyrenees—to one that becomes more and more of the
east. There are traces of the Moors even as far north as Burgos
and still more in Ávila—the lintel above the door into the
convent of the Incarnation is Moorish. At Toledo their civiliza-
tion has held its own with that of Hebrews, Romans, Crusaders,
Goths and Visigoths. But Córdoba, Seville and Granada, in
spite of centuries of Christianity, clanging church bells, way-
side shrines, monasteries and nunneries—in spite, too, of modern industries—to this day, it seems to me, belong to the Moors.
As I went through the empty echoing palaces walled with blue
and lemon *azulejos*, the hushed courtyards, the gardens cool
with fountains and rivulets and heavy with the scent of flowers,
I felt that the Moors had not gone away but were
sleeping.

Andalusia is a country of roses and giant violets, jasmine and
orange blossom; luxuriant, too, in vines and olives. Palms and
prickly pear give to it a look of the Levant. In summer, the
intense blue of the sky wearies the eyes. So does the pale dust
and the bone-like pallor of limestone rock. Houses are a blinding white; roofs, golden. Its people have soft Arab eyes and an
indolent Arab courtesy. They extend a more lavish welcome
than in Castile but forget more quickly. They have much wit,
less humour. They speak their Spanish with a lazy slur of
syllables. They are lovers of laughter, but quickly moved to
tears. They dance and sing, play the guitar, and array their
donkeys with tassels and brightly-coloured harness. Their
churches are darker than any I have seen, their Madonnas more
lavishly decked with brocades and jewels and rings. Their
Christs would move a heart of stone, yet have a primitive
savagery like the carvings of ancient Mexico.

In Seville, one evening, I had been looking at the statues in
the workshop of a carver in the Barrio de Santa Cruz. When I
came out into the dusk I asked the way of two nuns. As we
walked along one of them inquired where else in Spain I had

been. At the mention of Ávila, her face lit up. It was her native town. *'Bueno, bueno!'* she cried. *'Pero aquí, qué gente!'* she added scornfully with a shrug of her shoulders. The people of Seville had no dignity, she complained, and could not be relied on. After nearly four hundred years it was still the attitude of Teresa. Both she and John of the Cross had the Castilian's prejudice against the Andalusians. They were not, she said, her sort. 'It is amazing,' she writes to María Bautista, 'what wrongs are committed in this part of the world—what untruthfulness there is and double-dealing. I assure you, the place fully deserves its reputation.' And again: 'What falsehoods go round here! They make me quite dizzy.' In Andalusia, she says, God has given the devil greater power than elsewhere to tempt people.

The night falls quickly in Seville. Not as suddenly as in the east of the Mediterranean; yet suddenly enough for one to be reminded of Vergil's night that comes down, the poet says, with a rush. *Ruit nox.* The sky turns to a milky blue, like the petals of love-in-the-mist, then to a blue that is deep, yet luminous, in which the stars float like silver flowers. As the sky darkens, white walls become yet whiter and gates and balconies a deep black. Windows behind grilles make an amber glow. Water tumbling into a fountain basin is like silver hair. Under an archway a votive lamp flickers in front of a Christ wearing a cloak of crimson, a reed in his hand. Over all looms the cathedral black against the stars.

By day the cathedral used to remind me of a huge golden-brown animal crouching in the middle of the city. It would dwarf all else, were it not for the Giralda tower, standing at its side, giving elegance and lightness, lifting the whole city. I remember the interior of the cathedral in the early morning; a leafless wood in the dim light of the dawn. Great shadowy spaces reached on and up, and stained glass flung patterns of crimson, emerald, and gold on the giant pillars. People, standing or prostrating themselves or kneeling with arms outstretched, were dwarfed by the building's immensity. Footsteps and voices echoed feebly.

The Carmelite convent (it goes back to four years after Teresa's death) is a white building at the bend of a street in the Barrio de Santa Cruz. There is a painting of the saint high up on the wall with a lamp burning in front of it. In the little *patio* laden with the scent of jasmine and roses, a cat was sitting on a stone, blinking its golden eyes.

The Spaniards, disposed as they are to meditate on the transitoriness of life and the disintegration of the body, have a particular devotion to relics of the saints. Churches and convents treasure fragments of bone or withered flesh, decked with ribbon and enclosed in ornate gold or silver reliquaries that are exposed on altars or kept under lock and key, to be brought out for veneration on some feast day. I turned away in distaste from the relics at Alba de Tormes and from the ghoulish collections on view in glass cases at the Cartuja in Granada and in Seville Cathedral. On the other hand, those in the Seville convent are, mostly, in a different category. There is the white cloak Teresa was wearing up to the time of her death; a tubular crystal bottle given to her by the Duchess of Alba and used during her last illness; a drum; a hand-bell, called a *ronquita*, which she took with her on her travels; a copy of the Constitutions of the Incarnation as it was when she entered. There is, too, a sandal, sewn over with pearls by some devoted nun. Its small size brought to my mind Teresa's answer to a *caballero* who before she became a Carmelite was gazing in admiration at the neat foot just showing below her skirt: 'Have a good look, sir, for you won't get the chance again!' An ancient chronicler who saw her foot after her death said that it was like a piece of mother-of-pearl.

Most precious among the relics is the original manuscript of the *Interior Castle*, bound in silver that is inlaid with blue enamel and lined with crimson taffeta. For some years after Teresa's death it was in the possession of Gracián, who subsequently gave it to a certain Don Cerezo Pardo, a benefactor of the Carmelite monastery in Seville. His daughter, who became a nun, brought the manuscript with her to the convent as part of her dowry.

There are also two paintings, the work of Brother Juan de la Miseria whom I mentioned earlier as having joined the Reform at Pastrana. The first is a portrait of Teresa done at the request of her nuns before she left Seville in 1575. 'God forgive you, brother Juan! How ugly and blear-eyed you have made me!' was her comment on the finished picture. The words were spoken in fun. Later generations, however, have used them as an excuse to belittle a portrait which has much to commend it. Like many done during the same period in England, it has character and honesty. The hands, the dove and the scroll, all added later, can be ignored. The interest of the painting is in the face framed in the white coif and black veil. There is nothing sanctimonious about it. It is pleasing rather than beautiful; serene, not ecstatic. The dark eyes under the well-defined arched brows have a humorous, quizzical expression; they are eyes that see God; but they see man too—with a gentle, amused tolerance. Bernini has given us the Baroque Teresa: the visionary with rapturous gaze and flowing draperies caught up to heaven upon the clouds, the angel piercing her heart. Juan de la Miseria's Teresa is the saint who, while convinced of the truth of her visions, is forever questioning their validity, forever seeking assurance from those more learned than herself; who can laugh at herself and be prepared for her confessor to laugh too. '*¡ Qué San Pablo para ver cosas del cielo!*' Quite a Saint Paul with her heavenly experiences! This is the Teresa who travelled up and down Spain, slept in verminous inns, humoured mule-drivers and archbishops—a saint too natural for the Baroque world to understand; one who in the evidence for her canonization was remembered more for her kindness and gaiety than for her visions.

The second painting is of Lorenzo's daughter. It shows the

ten-year-old Teresita wearing the Carmelite habit. The face is
plump and smiling. The dark, intelligent eyes are the eyes
of Teresa.

*   *   *

The Hotel Inglaterra was comfortable in the solid Edwardian
tradition of cool spacious rooms with heavy furnishings and
plants in pots. Outside it in the Plaza Nueva yellow-wheeled
open carriages drawn by lean, well-cared-for horses stood
waiting to be hired. The drivers used to call out or wave a whip,
to attract a 'fare'. I can think of nothing more pleasant on a
summer night than to drive through the brightly lit streets,
then into the shadowy darkness of the eucalyptus trees and
hornbeams in the Parque de María Luisa and across the oil-
smooth river to the ancient suburb of Triana, where potters
and gypsies live and children dance on the pavement with wild
abandon. Teresa had a friend in Triana, Fernando de Pantoja,
Prior of the Carthusian monastery—a native of Ávila, of noble
birth. She calls him 'my prior'. 'How much I am indebted to
him for all his kindnesses!' she writes to María de San José. Also
at Triana was the Carmelite monastery called Los Remedios,
which played a large part in the history of the Reform.

In the centre of the Plaza Nueva there is a garden paved with
white marble and laid out with orange trees and palms. In the
evenings little boys in sailor suits and girls in crisp embroidered
dresses, their sleek dark hair tied up with ribbons, bowl their
hoops or skip, watched over by grave-faced nannies. Barely
a minute's walk from here, and in sight of the garden, is a quiet
street called the Calle de Zaragoza. Going along it one evening
I stopped outside the pillared porch of a white house that
curved with the curve of the street. The door stood open and
through a wrought iron gate I had noticed the *patio* with its
Moorish arches. I looked inside. On the wall facing me was a
tablet on which I read:

*Casa de Santa Teresa así llamada por haber morado en ella
conventualmente con las primeras religiosas de su fundación de
Sevilla la mistica Doctora, gloria de España, Reformadora
Insigne de la Orden del Carmen en el año de 1576.*

Saint Teresa's house; named thus because in 1576 there
dwelt here, together with the first nuns for this Seville
foundation, the great mystic who is the glory of Spain and
the Reformer of the Order of Carmel.

It was the house that Lorenzo found for Teresa on his return
from the New World. It had, she says, a fine garden and spacious
rooms off a *patio* that looked as if it were made of 'frosted
sugar'. Its situation was the finest in the city. In those days it
had an unbroken view to the river; Teresa valued this view. She
was indignant when, after she left Seville, María de San José
wanted to move to another house. Was it a small thing, Teresa
asked her, to be able to see the ships passing up and down? At
Malagón, the sisters had to live like lizards in a hole. She pointed
out, too, that the nuns might find it harder to pray, if deprived
of their view.

She had been overjoyed at the news of Lorenzo's return;
amazed, too, at the ways of God, that he should have brought
back to her 'those who had seemed so far away'. Hearing that
her brother and his children were at Sanlúcar de Barrameda
she wrote immediately, sending them some 'little things'. A
fortnight later they were in Seville, Lorenzo exhausted but
recovering, Teresita looking pretty.

Lorenzo's arrival and his kindness in finding the house
changed everything. Up to then there had been one difficulty
after another. When Teresa came to Seville in May, she found
the house that Mariano had taken for herself, and the six nuns
who were with her, damp and almost without furniture. It had
not occurred to him that bedding was necessary. Furthermore,
both he and Gracián had led her to suppose that Seville, being

a rich city, would be ready to provide anything that was
needed; that the Archbishop would be delighted at her coming; that there were young women only waiting to be taken
into the Order.

In fact, the city could hardly have been more apathetic. Apart
from Mariano, who did what he could to provide food and
money, there were no offers of help; no one brought so much
as a jug of water. There was opposition from the Franciscans,
and later from the Calced Carmelites. Then some irregularity
was found in the purchase deed of the house. Lorenzo, who was
the guarantor, had to go into hiding—he narrowly escaped
imprisonment. Finally there was a lawsuit in which the convent
lost. Nor was the Archbishop, Don Cristóbal de Rojas y
Sandoval, in any hurry to exert himself. 'All we have had to
endure since the foundation of Saint Joseph's,' Teresa writes,
when she has been eleven months in the city, 'has been nothing
as compared with what I have put up with here.' There were
moments when it seemed to her that God was withdrawing his
hand; when he seemed to be weary of her importunings. 'I
have heard you, let me be,' were Christ's words to her when
she kept begging for a house. As to the young women who
were waiting to become nuns, they decided that the Reform
was too austere. The difficulty of finding the right postulants
continued even after the foundation was well established. There
was particular trouble over *una beata grande*, a neurotic lady
who was 'a saint chiefly in her own estimation', whom the
convent had accepted under pressure from influential persons.
Finding that the life was not as she expected, she removed
herself—to the relief of all concerned—then proceeded to
denounce the community to the Inquisition. Among other
accusations, she said that the nuns were tied up by their hands
and feet and flogged. If all she said had been as silly, Teresa
comments, the matter would have been laughable.

Yet the time at Seville was not wholly unpleasant. If Teresa
did not care for the Andalusians, at least she was not troubled

as she used often to be in Castile by talk about her sanctity. 'I am allowed to live,' she says, 'and go about without being in terror that this ridiculous "tower of wind" will collapse over my head.' The climate, it is true, was trying. Yet even so in the middle of July she was able to tell her friend Don Antonio Gaytán that she and the nuns were well—that it was certainly hot but not as bad as on the journey from Beas. They had put up an awning, she said, in the *patio*. She enjoyed, too, the friendship of the Prior of Las Cuevas. It was, indeed, thanks to his wise counsel and tact that the convent was eventually founded. To honour the occasion there was a procession, in which clerics and confraternities took part. Salvoes of artillery were let off, and rockets. The crimson and yellow curtains in the chapel almost caught fire when some gunpowder was set alight by mistake. There were minstrels, coloured fountains, perfumes and orange-water. To crown all, when Teresa knelt before the Archbishop to ask his blessing, he fell on his knees begging hers in return. In short, the Discalced Carmelites suddenly found themselves honoured by everyone, though a while before all the water in the river would not have been enough to drown them.

*   *   *

From the time of the Seville foundation, Gracián is in the forefront of Teresa's letters. In two of them written from Seville to Juan Bautista Rubeo, General of the Carmelite Order, in an attempt to appease him with regard to the foundations made in Andalusia against his orders, she begs him ('women are not much good as counsellors, yet occasionally we are right') to listen to her pleas on behalf of his 'loyal sons' Gracián and Mariano: 'Let your Reverence remember that children are apt to err, and that fathers must not look at their faults, but forgive them.' Granted that Mariano, though well intentioned, is indiscreet—says much in fact that he does not mean, Gracián on the other hand 'behaves like an angel'; 'there is no one who has the gifts of this father.'

In spite of a life of continuous activity and an ever-widening circle of acquaintances and friends, Teresa, as she grew older, was sometimes lonely. She welcomed Gracián's company, was charmed by his gentleness and understanding. She admired him, too, for his intellect—she calls him 'a man of learning'; *hombre de muchas letras*. When she is at Toledo, she envies the nuns at Seville who have him with them. His welfare is a continual concern to her. She begs him to sleep enough, to put on warm clothes when the weather changes; to look after his chilblains. She is distressed because he has fallen off his mule— if his seat is not good, he would do well to be fastened on. 'I must tell you that I am cross about these falls you have been having. It would be as well if they were to tie you on to your mount, and then you would not fall. I don't know what sort of an animal you have nor why your Paternity has to do ten leagues a day: on a pack-saddle this is suicidal.' She sympathizes with him for having to eat 'cod patties'. She tells him that when he can, he should have his meals at the Seville convent. It would be unwise, however, to mention this to the friars at Los Remedios; as it is, she is worried because he has been visiting the convent in the company of an indiscreet brother, Andrés de los Santos, who is 'incapable of holding his tongue'. Well aware of an ingenuousness in Gracián's character which could too easily put him in a false position, she warns him against showing her letters to others: she writes to him with a frankness and warmth that could be misunderstood. Besides, it would not do if all nuns were to imagine that they could treat their Superior with the freedom that was possible between Gracián and herself. The thought that he is in Andalusia is a constant source of anxiety to her. This can be explained in part by her antipathy towards the Andalusians, but still more it is her fear of the Inquisition. A talented preacher, Gracián was constantly exposed to the public gaze; moreover, his predilection for mystical theology made him a likely target for those ready to suspect anyone interested in mysticism of being an Illuminist, and so a heretic. In the last year of her life she had a further cause for anxiety in the knowledge that there was an outbreak of plague at Seville.

Writing of prayer Teresa tells Gracián that he is to stop asking to be sent 'crosses', since when they come it is she who has to bear them. Experience has taught her that the most potent and most acceptable prayer is that which leaves the best effects—prayer, in short, which leads to action. This is true prayer, which is more than can be said of pious sensations which merely give pleasure to the person indulging in them. 'I should never want prayer that does not bring with it a growth in goodness. If, with my prayer, there come several temptations and aridities and tribulations and these leave me the more humble, then I would think it good. . . . One must not think that a person who is suffering is not praying. He is offering his sufferings to God, and often praying much more truly than someone who goes away by himself, meditates till he has a headache, squeezes out a few tears while imagining he is praying.' Suffering need not be feared; it cannot hurt the soul. She is amazed as she reads about the plagues of Egypt—how Moses was untouched by them: 'It is wonderful and delightful to see that, when the Lord so wills, there is nothing that has power to hurt us.' And again: 'I liked reading the passage about the Red Sea and reflected how much less we are asking of God than that. It made me glad, too, to see how that holy man came through all those adversities.'

*   *   *

Nicolás Doria was the man who after Teresa's death was to hound Gracián out of the Order. Saint John of the Cross—though at times so out of this world that as he walked along he would tap the wall with his knuckles to make sure he was still on earth—foresaw this would happen. He warned Gracián that Doria, if he became Provincial, would strip him of his habit.

In Teresa's writings the first mention of Doria is in connection with the Seville convent. It is in a letter to María de San José written from Toledo in September 1576, in which she says that she is reconsidering, obviously reluctantly, the question of a postulant recommended by Doria but thought unsuitable by herself and Gracián. She adds in a postscript that she has not dared to close the door on Nicolás altogether, the implication being (this is shown by other letters as well) that, as he was rich and influential, it might be unwise for so poor a convent not to defer to his wishes.

He belonged to a high-born family of Genoese bankers who had connections in Seville. After coming to Spain in 1570, he soon won prestige as banker to Philip, as well as for services in matters of finance to Archbishop Cristóbal Rojas y Sandoval. In the archives of the Discalced Carmelites in Rome there is the manuscript of a treatise on Exchange written by Doria. In March 1577, he disposed of his fortune to the poor and entered the Reform, receiving his habit a year later at the hands of Gracián.

Teresa had a high opinion of him. He was professed barely two months when, at a time critical for the Discalced, she was thinking of him as a suitable person to send to Rome on business to do with the Order. She describes him as humble and discreet, with a strict regard for the truth and able to win the goodwill of others. 'Father Nicolás spent three or four days with me in Ávila,' she writes to Gracián in July 1579. 'It was a great comfort to me to know your Paternity has someone now with whom you can discuss matters concerning the Order and who can help you in a way that gives me great satisfaction. It has worried me dreadfully to see you quite alone in the Order as you have been. I thought him really sensible and a good person to go to for advice and a servant of God, though he has not that graciousness and serenity that God has given to Paul (i.e.

Gracián).' She goes on to say that Doria recognizes Gracián's qualities, and is ready to follow him in everything. She was greatly pleased when, nearly three years later at the Chapter of Alcalá, Doria was appointed as *Socius*, or assistant, to Gracián who was now Provincial. 'I am delighted,' she writes in July 1579, 'that your Paternity has such a good companion.' What she wanted had come to pass. Doria, with his common sense, his experience of worldly affairs, was, she believed, the person best suited to help her Paul, who for all his gifts could on occasion be inconsequent, even indiscreet—was, moreover, regarded by the more extreme among the Discalced as being lacking in the firmness required of a Superior.

Teresa was mistaken. Doria, who was stern and unapproachable, was wholly out of sympathy with a temperament such as that of Gracián: he mistook the latter's ease of manner for familiarity and his disinclination to punish, if punishment could be avoided, for slackness. In fact, he had no understanding of the spirit as distinct from the letter of Teresa's Reform. Teresa with her sweeping breadth of vision saw the Rule laid down for her religious for what it was—a framework within which the spiritual life might be lived in community; a defence, too, against the whims and tyranny of intransigent superiors; commanding respect for the sake of those for whom it was made, not for itself; a means to an end, but not an end. It was the same regarding austerity. It, too, was no more than a means to an end, desirable only in so far as it detached the soul from self, leaving it free to love God. She says in a letter to Mariano de San Benito that men of talent whom it was her particular desire to bring into the Reform would be 'frightened off' by excessive austerity: *mucha aspereza se habían de espantar.*

Doria, on the other hand, who had neither Teresa's vision nor her largeness of heart, saw the good religious as someone living hour by hour meticulously by the letter of the Rule, occupied day in and day out in doing penance for his sins. His battle cry at the Chapter of Lisbon in 1585 was: 'Observance of the Rule ! Observance !' 'My bones in the grave,' he shouted, 'will still cry out "Observance".' Characteristic was his indignation when chicken appeared on the table at a meal served on the way to the Chapter of Almodóvar del Campo. Another time, when he was visiting a monastery, he was angered at hearing a book read which advocated discretion in matters of penance. These incidents occurred after Teresa's death, but there were hints of his attitude earlier. When he had been a friar only a short time, he showed signs of being obsessed with the idea that the Discalced had fallen away from their first fervour. He complained to Mariano, his friend and countryman, that he had been deceived in entering the Reform. He was scandalized at Alcalá de Henares in 1581, because the walls of the Chapter room were hung with Flemish tapestries.

Saint John of the Cross warned his Discalced brethren against ambition or greed for office, which he described as the most insidious of the vices, since it can be concealed behind actions that in themselves appear praiseworthy. Nicolás Doria was a man consumed by ambition. The energy that had gone to the making of the successful banker, the *habile brasseur d'affaires*, spurred him on now in the world of religion. He was a person who could not endure to be second, nor was he accustomed to such a role; already in the novitiate he had been singled out in preference to men older than himself to act on behalf of his Superior. In the Reform he knew that he would remain second as long as there was Gracián, the favourite of Teresa, whether as Provincial or merely a figure in the background. An excuse, then, must be found to get rid of Gracián. '*Doria a besoin de colorer son vice des apparences de la vertu.*'[1] So, to justify himself in the eyes of others but still more in his own, Doria built up the myth that the Discalced had become relaxed, laying the blame for this at the door of Gracián.

The full story of the conflict between these two is outside the

[1] *Le Conflit Doria-Gratien*, P. Hippolyte, O.D.C., p. 206. Also see Appendix, p. 182. (Note on the Reform.)

scope of this book. It is relevant, however, to ask how it was that Teresa, who was so shrewd in her judgment of human nature, should have been taken in—should have imagined that a partnership between Gracián and Doria could be possible, much less desirable. It would take a psychologist with all the facts at his disposal to answer this adequately.

Yet certain points stand out. First of all, it is probably true that there were times when Teresa, like most of us, saw people as she wanted to see them. She was, in any case, disposed to see the best in others. One has only to think of the numerous persons of whom she used such expressions as a 'good friend', a 'lover of perfection', a 'great servant of God'. She first knew Doria as a wealthy layman anxious to be of service to the Seville convent. Then, just when she wanted someone intelligent, practical and with a knowledge of the world, to help Gracián, Doria entered the Reform. When Teresa wanted anything, she did so, she says, with impetuosity. It is understandable, then, that she saw Doria's good qualities, but failed to see the power-striver with the ruthlessness characteristic of his kind. Like many who strive for power, he was careful at first not to reveal himself in his true colours. To have shown hostility to Gracián during Teresa's life would have been a tactical error. Instead, he played yet never overplayed (that, too, would have been fatal) the role of the humble friar anxious only to be at the disposal of the Reform, content in all things to be subject to Gracián. 'He will fully recognize how valuable Paul is,' Teresa writes, 'and is quite resolved to follow him in everything.'

Yet, there are hints that towards the end of her life—when it had become too late to alter a situation which she had herself to some extent created—Teresa was beginning to see the real Doria. Has she an inkling of a false humility that is nothing else than a cloak to conceal pride, when she writes to Nicolás hardly more than six months before her death: 'Your Reverence must not think that the art of governing consists in

merely hunting out our own sins. We must often forget ourselves altogether and remember that we hold office for God
and are carrying out his commands, that he will supply what we
lack, as he does to all, and that no one can be perfect. Do not
give way then to a misplaced humility.' There is reason, too,
to believe that it is to Doria she is referring when she writes to
Gracián: 'That other one who says everything must be done in
the way he wants has annoyed me.' There is no doubt whatever
that among the many worries during the last months of Teresa's
life not the least was the strained relations between these two
men. 'You badly need Nicolás,' she wrote to Gracián on September 1st, 1582, 'for I don't think you can possibly attend to so
many things at once.' Nicolás, however, was in Italy, acting
on Gracián's behalf. Being an Italian he would seem to have
been the obvious person to send. Nevertheless Teresa makes it
clear that his departure had given rise to gossip among a section
of the Reform who were already critical of Gracián. No doubt
they assumed that he had snatched at an opportunity to be rid
for a while of an uncongenial partner.

8

Burgos

I TRAVELLED back from Seville through the night to find in
Madrid a heat scarcely less intense than I had left behind in
Andalusia. Then I went to Toledo to look again at the *Entierro
del Conde de Orgaz*; it seemed more than ever like a vision
breaking upon the darkness of the church. Then, back to
Madrid. I had travelled enough, yet I had still not seen Burgos,
the place of Teresa's last foundation. The thought of another
journey was wearisome.

In fact, it was a restful one. My sole companion in the
railway carriage was an elderly Castilian, a carver of *imagenes*,
with a leather-brown furrowed face that he might have carved
himself. I looked out from the train at the walls of Ávila; then
at Arévalo and Medina and, after Medina, poplar trees and
birches, and on the horizon the flat-topped hills, going on, it
seemed, for ever—pale as ash, preparing the traveller for the
silver-grey stone of Valladolid and Burgos more silver still.

Burgos was bathed in light. It glittered on the cathedral's
twin spires and on the stone bridges across the Arlanzón. It was
not the blinding light of the south nor the pitiless light that
beats upon the Castilian plain. It was gentle, moving upon the
water with the movement of the wind, darting among the
leaves of chestnut trees already touched with the shrivelling
brown of autumn. There was dignity and peace in this city of
tree-lined streets, squares and fountains, steps leading up to
churches, Gothic spires. It brought to my mind a cathedral city
in France: in snow, I thought, it would look like an Utrillo
painting. And yet Burgos is predominantly Spanish. The Cid,
mounted on his charger, his cloak flying in the wind, looks on

to the bridge of San Pablo. His body lies under a slab of russet marble in a cathedral crammed with tombs, gilded screens, carvings, *retablos* and a wildly theatrical golden staircase. In the Casa del Cordón, so named from the Franciscan girdle that decorates its façade, Christopher Columbus was received by Queen Isabella on his return from his second voyage. A tree-shadowed road called the Calle de Muertes takes you along the river beyond the bounds of the city to Las Huelgas, the Cistercian nunnery founded by Eleanor, sister of Richard Coeur de Lion. Besides being the burial place of six kings and queens and as many as thirty royal children, it is a treasure house of jewelled robes, brocades and cloth of gold, crowns and coronets and coffins lined with silks of Arabia.

Teresa used to visit the nuns at Las Huelgas, proud ladies who in their strict seclusion still bore the title *Señora Doña*. She also visited Las Doroteas, who have an ancient thick-walled convent within the precincts of the city. A few minutes walk from the latter is the Hospital de la Concepción, a great shabby building decorated with renaissance carving, standing at a crossroads where lorries thunder past on their way to the south. Teresa and her nuns lived in the hospital for nearly two months while they were looking for a house. They were allotted a couple of rooms with a kitchen, on the top floor next to a disagreeable widow who, not content with having the communicating door locked, insisted upon it being nailed up as well. Later, they were given two more rooms lower down, to use as parlours. Gracián had an attic in which he used to say Mass on a platform. He was only allowed the room because no one would sleep in it; it was said to be full of hobgoblins. The patients were on the ground floor, in two wards; one for men and one for women. Teresa used to bring them oranges and limes hidden in the loose sleeves of her habit.

I saw the two convents and the hospital in the company of a grave and courteous citizen of Burgos who, one day when I was coming out of the priory of Los Padres Carmelitas, appeared as if from nowhere like an angel in the Bible or a character out of the *Foundations*—the young Andrada, for example, who helped Teresa in Toledo. He knew every stone of the city, but our progress was slow because at each church we came to—and they were many—he stopped to say a prayer. When we had seen all, I was taken to his home, where his wife laid before me as a delicacy a plate piled high with black shell-fish with great claws and whiskers. I tried to explain that, much as I appreciated the thought, I did not care for shell-fish. '*No puedo comer nada de mar,*' was all I could say. '*No son del mar, son del río, del río,*' husband and wife exclaimed in chorus, with expressions of dismay.

Teresa had wanted to come to Burgos less than I had. Indeed, she was almost relieved that there were obstacles which seemed to make a foundation, at that time, impossible. It was the winter of 1581. She was sixty-seven now, and not long back at Ávila from visiting convents she had founded at Palencia and Soria. The last two years had been hard ones. As well as one difficulty after another concerned with the Reform, in March 1580 she had suffered from a severe attack of *el catarro universal*—what we call influenza, but of a particularly virulent kind. Gracián's mother, also, had been ill, and her son Don Luis, and one of her daughters. The mother of John of the Cross had died. From that time, Teresa began to look an old woman. In June of the same year, while she was staying at Segovia and still unwell, news came to her of the death of her brother Lorenzo. 'You must know,' she wrote to María de San José, 'that our Lord has been pleased to take to himself his good friend and servant Lorenzo de Cepeda.' The shock was considerable. Only a fortnight before she had written, chiding him for letting himself imagine that he was going to die in the near future. 'I cannot think . . . why you have these ridiculous ideas or are oppressed by what will not happen.'

The obstacles in the way of the Burgos foundation began to disappear. A letter came, too, from her friend and benefactor

Doña Catalina de Tolosa, urging her to come quickly; there were other Orders thinking of making foundations and, charitable though the city was, there was a limit to the number of religious houses it could support. This was at the end of December, and the weather bitterly cold. There was snow on the ground. Could she stand the journey over the frozen, windswept plain? Then she heard Christ speaking to her: 'Have no thought for the cold. I am your warmth.'

*   *   *

On January 2nd, 1582, Teresa set out from the walls of Ávila for the last time. Gracián was with her, and two friars and three nuns, one of them Ana de San Bartolomé, who from the time that Teresa had broken her arm used to write letters for her, accompany her on her journeys and, when necessary, act as a nurse. All the way to Medina del Campo there was snow and rain. At Valladolid Teresa became so ill from a throat infection that the doctors advised her to leave the city at once. She went on to Palencia, a town for which she had a great affection. The people there, wanting to catch a glimpse of her and, if possible, ask her blessing, thronged round the mule-carts in such numbers that she had difficulty in getting out.

The worst part of the journey was to come. The floods were so bad that Gracián and the friars had to keep going on in front to find the road. Sometimes they had to help to drag the carts out of the mud. It was particularly bad at a ford outside Burgos called the Pontoons, where the water lay in immense sheets. A world of water, Teresa calls it. Gracián, who was usually of a placid disposition, was in a thorough fright. The carts were in constant danger of overturning, for the water had risen to such a height that the wooden bridges were covered—anyway, these were so narrow that the wheels of the vehicles could barely get on to them. The whole party made their confessions in preparation for death. They also recited the Creed. It was on this occasion that Teresa, old and ill as she was, made that dramatic gesture in keeping with the traditions of *Ávila de los Caballeros*. Urging her nuns to die, if need be, for the love of Christ, she went ahead of them into the water in the first cart. With characteristic common sense she told them however, that should she be drowned, the rest must return to the inn where they had passed the previous night. When they arrived at Burgos on January 26th, they found the streets like rivers.

The next day Teresa was so ill that she could not lift her head from the pillow. So as to be able to talk to the many persons, who called to see her, she had her bed put by a window opening on to a passage. They had reached Burgos soaked to the skin. Moreover, to make matters worse, instead of going straight to the house of Doña Catalina, their hostess, they had gone out of their way to see the miraculous Cristo de Burgos which was in the Augustinian church outside the bounds of the city. This had been planned beforehand by Gracián, whose common sense did not always match his intelligence. 'His Paternity does not want us to miss seeing the crucifix at Burgos and we are told we ought to visit it before entering the city,' Teresa had written to Doña Catalina from Palencia.

This crucifix, said to have been carved by Nicodemus and found floating on the sea in a box, is now in the cathedral where it was brought at the time of Napoleon's invasion. When I shall have forgotten all else in the city, I shall remember el Cristo de Burgos, I saw it for the first time in the evening, in the flickering light of tapers. Every now and again it was as though a shudder ran through the broken body. Any crucifix worthy of the name must stress a particular aspect of the Passion. It may be physical anguish, dereliction or majestic calm. The Burgos crucifix, with its human hair, its tortured emaciated body draped in a crimson skirt, has an agonizing primitive quality. This Christ would seem to have taken upon himself the dark, unspoken terror of primeval man; to be paying the price of blood shed on pagan altars or in secret groves.

Don Cristóbal Vela, formerly Bishop of the Canary Islands but at the time of which I write Archbishop of Burgos, was an exasperating, though by no means ill-intentioned man. Having given the impression to Teresa, as well as to their mutual friend the Bishop of Palencia, that nothing could please him more than that a Discalced convent should be founded in the city, he now took a different attitude. He had meant, he said with some heat, that she should come alone to talk things over, not bring a pack of nuns. The best thing they could do was to go back where they had come from—the quicker the better. ('The weather so delightful, too,' comments Teresa.) This mood lasted for over two months. Nothing would induce him to give a licence to found the convent. His city, he said, did not need to be reformed; its monasteries and convents were reformed enough already. Nor would he allow Mass to be said in Doña Catalina's house, though there was already a chapel there that had been used by the Jesuits. The nuns in their white cloaks and sandals had to walk through the wet muddy streets to hear Mass in the *Buena Mañana* chapel in the ancient church of San Gil. When His Grace was told that his behaviour had caused some of them to weep, he said they could go on weeping. The Bishop of Palencia, Gracián, and even the citizens of Burgos were exasperated by his attitude. One of the nuns was so irritated that merely to think of the Archbishop made her tremble.

Teresa remained calm. It was strange, she admitted, that His Grace did not realize, apparently, the inconvenience that he was causing. Beyond this not a word of criticism passed her lips. 'Sometimes,' she writes in the *Foundations*, 'I would regret the things I heard being said about him more than those that were happening to ourselves.' When she paid him a visit and still achieved nothing, she came away in good spirits, saying that she had much enjoyed the talk. She even went so far as to refer to him as a 'saint'. Her calm was more than a mask. By now she was long inured to opposition and confident that with patience it could be overcome. 'Things are going much as they did in Seville. This turmoil and opposition will do us no harm,' she writes to María de San José. She sees the difficulties as an advertisement which will ultimately be beneficial to the Reform. If all had gone well, the Discalced would not have been noticed. As it is, even before the convent is founded, postulants are clamouring to be admitted.

The situation had much in common with that of Seville. In Seville Don Cristóbal Rojas y Sandoval, after opposing Teresa, had knelt at her feet. In Burgos Don Cristóbal Vela eventually called on her. When he expressed a wish for a jug of water, Teresa begged him to accept a small gift that had been made to her. He was disarmed. 'I have never,' he said, 'accepted any such thing from anyone in Burgos. But I accept it because it is from you.' Even so he did not immediately grant the licence. However, he did grant it at last. Further, he was himself present on the occasion of the first Mass, when he embarrassed everyone by expressing his remorse at having been the cause of so long a delay. He then went on to declare his affection and admiration for the Foundress. To add to the rejoicings of that day, minstrels came unasked and accompanied the Mass with 'most solemn music'.

This was in April 1582, in the convent dedicated to Saint Joseph and Saint Ann that I could see from my window. It stood there four-square by the river, on the edge of the city. Its stone walls were pale in the sunlight; pale, too, under the stars. Beyond, there were trees and, further still, the plain. It seemed to me fitting that Teresa should have made her last foundation in this city of kings in the north of Castile—as though she were already looking beyond her own land to the time, soon to come, when her daughters would be founding houses of the Reform in France and the Netherlands and England.

9

Alba de Tormes

'*Señor mio, ya es tiempo de caminar; sea muy enhorabuena y cumplese vuestra santísima voluntad.*'
My Lord, it is now time to set out. I do so gladly. May your most holy will be done.

When Teresa left Burgos at the end of July 1582 she was planning a foundation in Madrid. In fact, her work was ended. I mean her active work; for after the body has done its part, the work of the soul, that mysterious purgation of self known only to God, goes on into the hour of death.

From Burgos she went with Ana de San Bartolomé and her niece Teresita to Palencia; then on to Valladolid, where she was drawn reluctantly into business relating to Lorenzo's will. 'You would be shocked if you knew all the trouble I am having here, and all the business I have to do—it is killing me,' she writes to Ana de los Ángeles at Toledo. Doña Beatriz de Castilla, mother-in-law of Lorenzo's son Francisco (Teresa calls her 'a strange woman') wanted the will to be proved invalid. She was particularly vindictive towards Teresa. So was the lawyer, who when he called to see her told her that she, a nun, had behaved as no lady should. Teresa answered him gently with an irony that would be lost on any but the sensitive: 'May God reward you, Señor, for your charity.'

The Prioress of the Valladolid convent, influenced perhaps by Doña Beatriz who was considered a woman of some standing, also turned against Teresa. This was María Bautista, formerly María de Cepeda y Ocampo—the young cousin who had been one of the first to embrace the Reform, the girl whom

Teresa had befriended years before at Ávila, taking her to live
at the Incarnation when she had been left homeless after her
mother's death and her father's second marriage. Indeed,
Teresa had been a friend to María Bautista all her life, giving
her wise counsel and bearing with her moods. Ana de San
Bartolomé, who tells what happened at Valladolid, does not
mince her words. 'She told us,' she says of María Bautista, 'to
leave her convent. Then, when we were going out the door,
she caught hold of my habit and said, "Be gone, the two of you,
and don't come back again".'

While she was at Valladolid Teresa wrote to the Prioress of
Burgos asking her to put up with the vagaries of Doña Catalina
de Tolosa, who had given hospitality and help to the Discalced
while making their foundation in that city. 'Do not be shocked
at Catalina de Tolosa. She is so overworked that you ought
rather to comfort her; she may say one thing today, then do
quite another tomorrow.' She begs her, too, not to saddle her
novices with too many duties: 'Your Reverence thinks that all
the nuns have as much determination as yourself, but in that
you are greatly mistaken.' Apart from a casual mention of
'trials', there is nothing in the letter about her own troubles.
Writing to Gracián, on the other hand, five days later she makes
no attempt to hide what she feels. She has had a 'perfectly
wretched' night. Her head aches: she hopes it will be better the
next day when the moon will be past its full. She has had a
dreadful time, too, with Don Francisco's mother-in-law about
the validity of the will. Worst of all Gracián, when she most
needs him, has gone away. So keenly had she felt his going that
she lost even the inclination to write. Besides, Teresita is
disappointed that he will not be at Ávila for her profession:
'In one way I am glad; she will begin to understand how little
trust one can place in anyone except God—it has done me no
harm either.' As always she is full of concern for Gracián's
welfare. She hopes he is not letting himself be bullied by a
determined Prioress at Salamanca who is set on buying a house

that is too large—and far too expensive: 'For the love of God, your Reverence, think very carefully what you are doing. Do not pay too much attention to what nuns say. I can assure you that if they want a thing they will find a thousand arguments.' She is concerned above all because he has gone to Andalusia; 'I never like it when your Reverence is there for long. . . . Don't think of turning yourself into an Andalusian; you are not of the temperament to live among them. As for your sermons there, I earnestly beg your Reverence once again to be very careful what you say, even though you preach only rarely.'

*   *   *

In the middle of September Teresa travelled south to Medina del Campo over the solitary distances of the plain with its landscapes of stubble and ochre earth, poplar trees and flat-topped hills, their ashen pallor reflecting the purple and crimson of the evening sky. She was tired. But she would rest at Medina in the convent in the Calle de Santiago, then go on to Ávila to be at Saint Joseph's for Teresita's profession.

There was no rest at Medina. Antonio de Jesús was waiting with instructions that, instead of going direct to Ávila, she was to make a detour to Alba de Tormes; the Duchess had sent her coach asking that she should come immediately to be with her daughter-in-law, the Duchess of Huesca, who was waiting to give birth to a child. The evening before Teresa set out, there was a difference of opinion with the Prioress, Alberta Bautista, who flounced out of the room. What Teresa would have turned off with a laugh when she was well hurt her now. She did not eat her supper that night nor could she sleep.

It is a long lonely road from Medina to Alba de Tormes. In the evening, when they came to a village called Cantaracello near Peñaranda, Teresa was so ill that Ana de San Bartolomé feared she would die. They could not get so much as an egg to eat—only dried figs, and on the next day in another village cabbage cooked in onion. They were approaching Alba de

Tormes when they were met with the news that the Duchess of Huesca had been delivered of a child. 'So "the saint" won't be needed,' Teresa remarked. She was so exhausted when she reached the convent that she let the nuns put her to bed. 'God help me,' she said, 'how tired I am! I haven't been to bed so early for years.'

That was on September 20th. On October 4th she died.

*   *   *

I do not know a place more peaceful than Alba de Tormes. Pilgrims are few, the convent chapel silent. The basilica planned in Teresa's honour is unfinished; there are only the walls—as though the saint would have nothing of this transient splendour. Quiet streets of houses that are a shabby white or brown like sand, with blinds and balconies and sometimes a coat of arms carved above a doorway, drop gently to where the broad placid river slips under the many-arched Roman bridge, mirroring the poplar trees by day and at night the stars. Swallows skim the water. Oxen come down to drink. Women kneeling on the bank wash clothes, then spread them on the stones to dry as the women of Alba have done since the town's beginning. It is a gracious river, loved of poets: Garcilaso sang of it, and Lope de Vega and Calderón. Luis de León used to meditate by its waters, and when he was in prison wrote of it in elegant lilting periods.

Alba de Tormes is a town of many convents, many churches. In the ancient parish church of San Pedro there hangs el Cristo de la Salud, a desolate Christ with bowed head and hair that falls to the waist as if to veil the tortured body. There is a legend that during a flood this crucifix was swept away as far as Ledesma, and that the inhabitants of that town, believing this to have happened providentially, were reluctant to give it back. The fathers at San Pedro prayed that a solution might be found. Shortly after, two strangers came one evening asking for lodging. In the morning they had vanished, leaving behind them a replica of the lost crucifix. There is, too, the church of San Juan where the Twelve Apostles and their Master, carved in stone with a rigid Byzantine formalism and painted in faded colours that are like the reflection thrown from stained glass, sit staring in front of them with expressions that are a mixture of gravity and mild surprise. The pulpit in this church bears the arms of the town; the castle and bridge and river; above the bridge two stars and in the water below a third star.

*   *   *

It is fitting that Teresa did not end her life at Ávila. The saints, like ourselves, have their roots in the place of their birth, bear the mark of that place and shed glory on it. The spirit of Ávila lives in Teresa, while she in turn has lifted her city from being an historical monument to become a name revered wherever man's experience of the divine has meaning. The same may be said of Saint Thomas and Aquino, Saint Francis and Assisi, Saint Thèrese and Lisieux. The saints belong to these places and yet have outgrown them—not as anyone outgrows the environment of childhood, but to the extent that they belong to no one place, which is to say they belong everywhere because they belong to God.

It is fitting, too, that she died at Alba de Tormes, a place so tranquil that it is itself a symbol of that peace of soul to which after long conflict she attained. It was a town for which she had a particular affection. She used to find it restful. Not that this was always so. There were worries over her sister's family and from time to time troubles in the convent. Even so, for Teresa Alba was a place of peace. In a letter to the Prioress at Salamanca—it was accompanied by a trout to be given to a Dominican theologian—she says that she wishes she could enjoy the pleasures of Salamanca and Alba at the same time. She is delighted by the view of the river from a hermitage in the garden. She can also see the river from her cell as she lies in bed. Teresa had always loved water. It was at once useful,

mysterious and beautiful. 'What would become of the world
if there were no water for washing?' she exclaims in the *Way
of Perfection* when considering the properties of water. She
reflects, too, how strange it is that, though it has the power to
put out a fire, yet if there is tar in the fire water only makes it
burn the more violently; she wishes that she could discuss this
with some man of learning. Besides all else, water is a symbol of
God's grace. It is the image that she uses more than any other
in her spiritual writings. Discoursing in the *Life* on the four
degrees of prayer, she recalls the ways in which an orchard can
be watered. The water can be brought from a well at the cost of
much toil, or it can be drawn by a windlass—she remembers
having drawn it this way herself: or there may be a stream nearby, which means less labour. But it is best of all when the Lord
sends down the rain from heaven, soaking the earth. In the
Way of Perfection she writes of the source of Living Water at
which all are invited to drink—the source of streams and rivulets, some great, some small, and of little pools for children who
else would be frightened at the sight of so much water. The
pleasure she found in looking at water remained with her the
whole of her life. Writing to Gracián in June 1581, she envies
him for being at the Salamanca monastery which has a view
on to the Tormes. In a letter of the following September to
Don Jerónimo Reinoso, a friend who helped her with the
Palencia foundation, she says that her journeys are 'dreadfully
tiring', yet the one from Palencia to Soria has been the reverse
(she calls it a *recreación*) because all the way along the road there
were glimpses of the river keeping her company; *que me hacían
harta compañía.*

Growth in grace had not made Teresa less human. She had
not become blind to the world of nature or a Simon Stylites
remote from her fellows. She used to say that, if a friend's head
ached, her own ached too—so much did people matter to her.
It remained so to the end. That was why she minded the harsh-
ness of María Bautista and Alberta Bautista, and the absence of

Gracián. She had remained fastidious, too, as in the old days at
Ávila when she had taken trouble with her hands and her hair
and liked perfumes. She was fussed in her last illness, when the
Duchess of Alba, who used to visit her and feed her with her
own hand, chanced to call after some strong-smelling medicine
had been spilt on the sheet. She was afraid the Duchess might be
offended. She need not have been anxious. Those who were
with her said that the room smelt as if it had been sprinkled
with water from heaven; *con agua de ángeles.* Nor to the end
did she lose her gift of repartee. Asked whether she wanted to
be buried at Ávila, she replied: 'Can't they spare a handful of
earth here?' It was like her not to care about the place of her
burial. Her thoughts were on life, not death. Life eternal, yet
life in this world too. The time was drawing near for her niece's
profession. She must not disappoint Teresita, 'a good little
thing, but hardly more than a child': *aunque es bonita es niña, en
fin.* A few days before she died, she said to Ana de San Bartolomé: 'As soon as I'm better, get me a cart and we'll go to
Ávila—the three of us.' *Vamos a Ávila.*

They will wait for you in vain in Ávila, Teresa. In the villages they will not see the mule-carts pass. They will not see
you any more in Medina or Toledo, Seville or Salamanca,
Burgos or Valladolid. Have no fear, María Bautista, the
Foundress will not come again. The great ladies of Madrid
need not hope to catch a glimpse of you. Nor will stern Philip
smile to read your letters. All this is ended now, for all things
pass;

> *Todo se pasa*
> *Dios no se muda*

Yet they will remember you. They will forget the bishops and
the archbishops, the theologians and the Grand Inquisitor, but
they will remember the nun in the patched habit who was gracious and gay and had no use for long-faced saints. And others
coming after in other countries and in another age will marvel,

looking back across the centuries, at how this woman, who while still on earth had foretaste of the joys of heaven, was no less human than themselves.

You have come to the end of your journey, Teresa, and I to the end of mine. Night has fallen at Alba de Tormes. A wind stirs in the poplar trees and the river carries the stars.

Appendix

TERESA'S COUSINS
(*See page* 23)
Padre Efrén de la Madre de Dios, O.D.C., in his *Biografía de Santa Teresa* describes the sons of Doña Elvira as '*hidalgos y ricos*' born in the years 1507, 1508 and 1513. He points out that at the time when Teresa says she was going about with her cousins the eldest of Don Francisco's sons could not have been more than six or seven years old.

See *Obras de Santa Teresa. Biblioteca de Autores Cristianos.* Vol. 1, page 283.

THE NUNS IN THE CONVENT OF THE INCARNATION
(*See page* 38)
The nuns in the convent of the Incarnation are Discalced Carmelites, that is followers of the Reform introduced by Saint Teresa. This, however, is only since the year 1940. Up till then they were Calced Carmelites as in Teresa's own day. (For the significance of the word Discalced see Chapter 3, page 78)

THE REFORM
(*See page* 78)
The complicated history of Teresa's Reform is described in the *Handbook to the Life and Times of St. Teresa and St. John of the Cross* by Allison Peers. There is also an important and interesting Postscript by Fr Benedict Zimmerman, O.D.C., in *St. John of the Cross* by Fr Bruno, O.D.C. For the part played by Gracián and Doria see *Le Conflit Doria-Gratien* by P. Hippolyte, O.D.C., an historical and psychological study in which justice is done to the often maligned and misunderstood Gracián, while Doria, the revered 'Lion of Carmel' is shown to have been a bully and a power-striver.

'WE NEED ALL THIS TO MAKE LIFE LIVABLE'
(*See page* 83)
There is a strong tradition of song and dance among the Discalced Carmelites of Spain. Teresa and John of the Cross are mentioned on several occasions as singing and dancing. Teresa, too, defended the Franciscan, Peter of Alcántara, when people said he was mad because

he used to go through the fields singing to himself. 'May God give us all that kind of madness!' she said. When Ana de Jesús began to make foundations outside Spain after Teresa's death she astonished the nuns in France by dancing in the choir and clapping her hands in the traditional Spanish manner.

For a detailed study of this subject see *Poesía Tradicional Carmelitana* by Emilio Orozco Díaz. Madrid. 1956.

Chronology

1515 Birth of Teresa de Cepeda y Ahumada

1519 Birth of her brother Lorenzo

1520 Birth of her brother Antonio

1521 Birth of her brother Pedro

1522 Teresa sets out for the land of the Moors with her elder brother Rodrigo

1528 Birth of her sister Juana
Death of her mother Doña Beatriz de Ahumada

1531 Teresa goes as a boarder to the convent of Our Lady of Grace

1536 Teresa enters the Carmelite convent of the Incarnation as a novice

1543 The death of her father Don Alonso Sánchez de Cepeda

1562 The foundation of Saint Joseph's, the first convent of the Reform

1565 Teresa completes the *Life* and begins the *Way of Perfection*

1567 Padre Juan Bautista Rubeo, General of the Carmelite Order, visits Teresa at Ávila. He authorizes her to found further convents, also two houses for friars
Foundation of convent at Medina del Campo

1568 Foundation of convents at Malagón and Valladolid
Foundation of monastery at Duruelo

1569 Foundation of convents at Toledo and Pastrana
Foundation of monastery at Pastrana

1570 Foundation of convent at Salamanca

1571 Foundation of convent at Alba de Tormes
Teresa becomes Prioress at the convent of the Incarnation

1573 Teresa writes her first letter to Philip II and begins the book of the *Foundations*

1574 Foundation of convent at Segovia

1575 Teresa meets Padre Gracián for the first time
Foundation of convents at Beas and Seville

1577 Teresa writes the *Interior Castle*

1580   Death of Lorenzo de Cepeda
        Foundation of convents at Villanueva de Jara and Palencia
1581   Foundation of convent at Soria
1582   Foundation of convent at Burgos
        Teresa dies at Alba de Tormes
1622   Teresa is canonized by Pope Gregory XV

Bibliography

SAINT TERESA'S OWN WRITINGS

Obras de Santa Teresa de Jesús. Editadas y anotadas por el P. Silverio de Santa Teresa, O.D.C. Tipografía 'El Monte Carmelo'. Burgos. 1915-1924. 9 vols.

Obras de Santa Teresa de Jesús. Edición y notas del P. Silverio de Santa Teresa O.D.C. Tipografía 'El Monte Carmelo'. Burgos. 1922.

Obras de Santa Teresa de Jesús. Estudio preliminar y notas explicativas por Luis Santullano. Aguilar Madrid. 1951.

Santa Teresa de Jesús; Obras Completas. Edición preparada por los Padres Fr. Efrén de la Madre de Dios O.D.C. y Fr. Otilio del Niño Jesús O.D.C. Vols. I and II. Biblioteca de Autores Cristianos. Madrid. 1951.

The Life of St. Teresa of Jesus. Tr. David Lewis. Notes and introd. by the Very Rev. Benedict Zimmerman, O.D.C. Thomas Baker. 1911.

The Way of Perfection. Tr. by the Benedictines of Stanbrook. With introduction and notes by the Very Rev. Benedict Zimmerman, O.D.C. Thomas Baker. London. 1911.

The Book of the Foundations, with the Visitation of Nunneries, the Rule and Constitutions. Tr. David Lewis. With introduction by the Very Rev. Benedict Zimmerman, O.D.C. Thomas Baker. London. 1913.

The Interior Castle; or the Mansions and Exclamations of the Soul to God. Tr. by the Benedictines of Stanbrook. With introduction and notes by the Very Rev. Benedict Zimmerman, O.D.C. Thomas Baker. London. 1921.

The Letters of St. Teresa. Tr. and annotated by the Benedictines of Stanbrook, with an introduction by Cardinal Gasquet. Thomas Baker. London. 1919-24.

The Complete Works of Saint Teresa of Jesus. Tr. and edited by E. Allison Peers from the critical edition of P. Silverio de Santa Teresa, O.D.C. Sheed and Ward. London. 1944-46. 3 vols.

The Letters of Saint Teresa of Jesus. Tr. and edited by E. Allison Peers from the critical edition of P. Silverio de Santa Teresa, O.D.C. Burns, Oates & Washbourne Ltd. London. 1951. 2 vols.

OTHER RELEVANT WORKS

Acta Sanctorum: *Acta S. Teresiae a Jesu* illustrata a Josepho Vandermölke. Bruxellis. 1845.

Bruno, Fr., O.D.C.: *St. John of the Cross.* Edited by Fr. Benedict Zimmerman, O.D.C., with an introduction by Jacques Maritain. Sheed and Ward. London. 1937.

Bruno, P.: *L'Espagne Mystique.* Arts et Métiers Graphiques. Paris. 1946.

Crisógono de Jesús, P., O.D.C.: *The Life of Saint John of the Cross.* Translated by Kathleen Pond. Longmans. 1958.

Díaz, Emilio Orozco: *Poesía Tradicional Carmelitana.* Estudios dedicados a Menéndez Pidal. Madrid. 1956.

Fortunato de J. Sacramentado, P., O.D.C.: *Medicina y Posesión Diabólica.* Revista de Espiritualidad. Abril–Junio. 1957.

Goldscheider, Ludwig: *El Greco.* Phaidon Edition. George Allen & Unwin. London. 1938.

Hernández, Ferreol: *Santa Teresa de Ávila.* Senén Martín. Ávila. 1952.

Hippolyte, P., O.D.C.: *Le Conflit Doria-Gratien.* Études Carmélitaines le 25 Mai 1948. Desclée de Brouwer. Paris.

Hoornaert, Abbé Rodolphe: *Saint Teresa in her Writings.* Tr. Rev. J. Leonard. Sheed and Ward. London. 1931.

Joly, H.: *Saint Teresa.* Tr. E. M. Waller. R. & T. Washbourne. London. 1913.

Lepée, Marcel: *Sainte Thérèse de Jésus et le Démon.* Études Carmélitaines le 25 Mai 1948. Desclée de Brouwer. Paris.

Luis de San José, O.D.C.: *Concordancias de las obras y escritos de Santa Teresa de Jesús.* Tipografía 'El Monte Carmelo'. Burgos. 1945.

Maugham, W. Somerset: *Don Fernando.* Heinemann. London. 1935.

Peers, E. Allison: *Handbook to the Life and Times of St. Teresa and St. John of the Cross.* Burns & Oates. 1954.

Peers, E. Allison: *Studies of the Spanish Mystics.* Sheldon Press. London. 1927–30. 2 vols.

Ribera, Francisco de: *Vida de Santa Teresa de Jesús.* Librería de Francisco Lizcano. Madrid. 1863.

Silverio de Santa Teresa, P., O.D.C. *Historia del Carmen Descalzo.* Tipografía 'El Monte Carmelo'. Burgos, 1935–49. 14 vols. (the first four volumes).

Silverio de Santa Teresa, P., O.D.C. *Procesos de Beatificación y Canonización de Sta. Teresa de Jesús.* Tipografía 'El Monte Carmelo'. Burgos. 1935. 4 vols.

INDEX